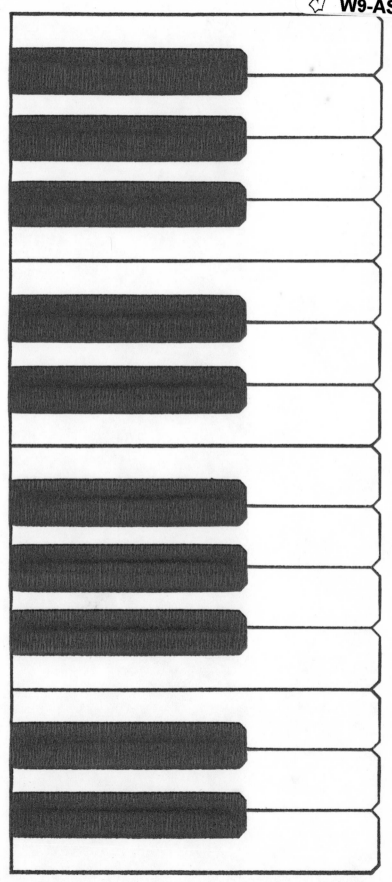

SILVER BURDETT

music

ELIZABETH CROOK
BENNETT REIMER
DAVID S. WALKER

SILVER BURDETT COMPANY

MORRISTOWN, NEW JERSEY   ·   GLENVIEW, ILLINOIS
PALO ALTO   ·   DALLAS   ·   ATLANTA

SPECIAL CONTRIBUTORS

William M. Anderson (non-Western music), Aurora, Ohio

Kojo Fosu Baiden (music of Africa), Silver Springs, Maryland

Dulce B. Bohn (recorder), Wilmington, Delaware

Charles L. Boilès (music of Mexico), Bloomington, Indiana

Ian L. Bradley (Canadian music), Victoria, British Columbia, Canada

Gerald Burakoff (recorder), Levittown, New York

Henry Burnett (music of Japan), Flushing, Long Island, New York

Richard J. Colwell (testing and evaluation), Urbana, Illinois

Marilyn C. Davidson (music for Orff instruments), Bergenfield, New Jersey

Joan Davies (music of Canada and Japan), Charlottetown, P.E.I., Canada

Kay Hardesty (special education), Chautauqua, New York

James M. Harris (music in early childhood), San Francisco, California

Doris E. Hays (avant-garde music), New York City

Nazir A. Jairazbhoy (music of India), Windsor, Ontario, Canada

Maria Jordan (music of Greece), Hicksville, Long Island, New York

Robert A. Kauffman (music of Africa), Seattle, Washington

Edna Knock (music of Canada), Brandon, Manitoba, Canada

John Lidstone (visual arts), Brooklyn, New York

David McHugh (youth music), New York City

Alan P. Merriam (music of the North American Indians), Bloomington, Indiana

Lucille Mitchell (American folk songs), Alexandria, Virginia

Maria Luisa Muñoz (music of Puerto Rico), Houston, Texas

Lynn Freeman Olson (listening program), New York City

Mary E. Perrin (music in the inner city), Chicago, Illinois

Carmino Ravosa (children's song literature), Briarcliff Manor, New York

Joyce Bogusky-Reimer (avant-garde music), Wilmette, Illinois

Geraldine Slaughter (music of Africa), Washington, D.C.

Mark Slobin (music of the Near East), Middletown, Connecticut

Ruth Marie Stone (music of Africa), New York City

Leona B. Wilkins (music in the inner city), Evanston, Illinois

CONSULTANTS

Lynn Arizzi (levels 1 and 2), Reston, Virginia

Joy Browne (levels 5 and 6), Kansas City, Missouri

Nancy Crump, classroom teacher, Alexandria, Louisiana

Lyla Evans, classroom teacher, South Euclid, Ohio

Catherine Gallas, classroom teacher, Bridgeton, Missouri

Linda Haselton, classroom teacher, Westminster, California

Ruth A. Held, classroom teacher, Lancaster, Pennsylvania

Judy F. Jackson, classroom teacher, Franklin, Tennessee

Mary E. Justice, Auburn University, Auburn, Alabama

Jean Lembke (levels 3 and 4), Tonawanda, New York

Barbara Nelson, classroom teacher, Baytown, Texas

Terry Philips (youth music), New York City

Ruth Red, Director of Music Education, Houston, Texas

Mary Ann Shealy (levels 1 and 2), Florence, South Carolina

Beatrice Schattschneider (levels 1–6), Morristown, New Jersey

Paulette Schmalz, classroom teacher, Phoenix, Arizona

Sister Helen C. Schneider, Clarke College, Dubuque, Iowa

Merrill Staton (recordings), Alpine, New Jersey

ACKNOWLEDGMENTS

The authors and editors of SILVER BURDETT MUSIC acknowledge with gratitude the contributions of the following persons.

Marjorie Hahn, New York

Yoriko Kozumi, Japan

Ruth Merrill, Texas

Bennie Mae Oliver, Texas

Joanne Ryan, New York

Helen Spiers, Virginia

Mary Ann Nelson, Texas

Shirley Ventrone, Rhode Island

Avonelle Walker, New York

Credit and appreciation are due publishers and copyright owners for use of the following.

"City" from GOLDEN SLIPPERS by Langston Hughes. Copyright © 1958 by Langston Hughes. Reprinted by permission of Harold Ober Associates, Inc.

"Fourth of July Night" from COMPLETE POEMS by Carl Sandburg. Copyright 1950 by Carl Sandburg. Reprinted by permission of Harcourt Brace Jovanovich, Inc.

"Summer Grass" from GOOD MORNING, AMERICA, copyright 1928, 1956 by Carl Sandburg. Reprinted by permission of Harcourt Brace Jovanovich, Inc.

"Swift Things Are Beautiful" reprinted with permission of The Macmillan Company from AWAY GOES SALLY by Elizabeth J. Coatsworth. Copyright 1934 by The Macmillan Company, renewed 1962 by Elizabeth Coatsworth Beston.

CONTENTS

SECTION 1

INTRODUCTION TO RHYTHM

Sounds give us a feeling of movement. The movement of sounds in music is called *rhythm*. This section will explore many of the ways that rhythm works in music.

Paintings can also give us a feeling of movement, even though nothing is actually moving.

Which of the paintings, by the same artist, gives more feeling of stillness?
Which gives more feeling of movement? Why?

MIRO: DOG BARKING AT THE MOON

MIRO: CARNIVAL OF HARLEQUIN

SWIFT THINGS ARE BEAUTIFUL

Swift things are beautiful:
Swallows and deer,
And lightning that falls
Bright-veined and clear,
Rivers and meteors,
Wind in the wheat,
The strong-withered horse,
The runner's sure feet.

And slow things are beautiful:
The closing of day,
The pause of the wave
That curves downward to spray,
The ember that crumbles,
The opening flower,
And the ox that moves on
In the quiet of power.

Elizabeth J. Coatsworth

Poems have movement also. How is fast and slow movement created in this poem?

What are the swift things mentioned in the first stanza?

What are the slow things mentioned in the second stanza?

As you read the poem again, feel the fast or slow movement of what your mind "sees."

Artists and designers can give a feeling of movement by the way they make things look. How has the artist given a feeling of movement to this airplane?

USING WHAT YOU KNOW ABOUT RHYTHM
Steady Beat/Meter in 2

Rhythm is a combination of many qualities—beat, tempo, meter, and rhythm patterns.

Show the steady beat in this folk song by making up your own hand-clapping and finger-snapping pattern. Take turns doing your motions while others sing.

MAMA DON'T 'LOW   AMERICAN FOLK SONG

📖 For recorder parts, see p. 207.

📖 For more practice feeling the steady beat, see p. 222.

Find the G, C, and D$_7$ chords on the Autoharp. The letters above each line of music will tell you which chord to play to accompany the singing.

First play the steady beat as in number 1 below. Then try to play one of the other rhythm patterns.

To accompany the singing on a guitar, find the G and the D strings. The photograph will help you. Pluck the single string on the steady beat, in one of the rhythm patterns shown above, or in a pattern of your own. Play G for both the G and C chords.

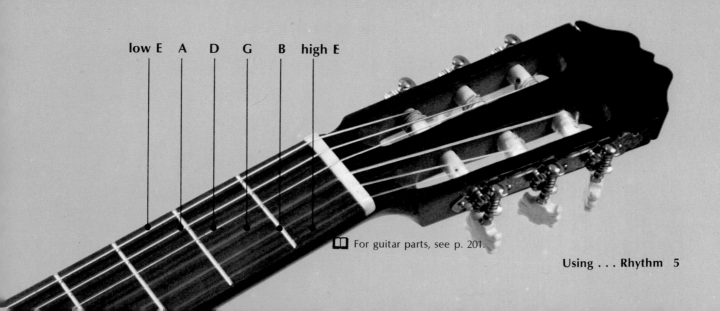

low E A D G B high E

For guitar parts, see p. 201.

Tempo/Meter in 2

This block-passing game from Africa changes tempo.

Before playing the game, listen to the chant. Does the tempo get faster, or slower?

SASA AKROMA   SINGING GAME FROM AFRICA

FROM AFRICAN SONGS AND GAMES FOR CHILDREN COMPILED AND TRANSCRIBED BY KOJO FOSU BAIDEN AND GERALDINE SLAUGHTER. © 1970. KOJO FOSU BAIDEN AND GERALDINE SLAUGHTER.

Sah   sah kroh mah   woh nay   ah   woh chay chay nkoh koh mah.

Sah   sah kroh mah   woh nay   ah   woh chay chay nkoh koh mah.

Any number can play. Players sit in a circle. Each player holds a block of wood.

Use only one hand throughout the game. On the strong beats (marked with an *X*), place your block in front of the player on your right. On the weak beats, pick up the block that has been placed in front of you.

Keep the blocks moving. If you miss a beat, or drop or throw a block, you're out!

Your two motions—pass and pick up—show the beats moving in twos. Notice the top number in the meter signature of the song. Feel the meter as you sing without moving.

For another block-passing game, see p. 239.

6 Using . . . Rhythm

Meter in 4

Sandy Ree is a favorite dance of the West Indies. The basic step shows beats in 4. The dance is done with a sideways step and a "chug" on the fourth beat of each measure. (A "chug" is a hop backward without the foot leaving the floor.)

Sandy Ree may be danced alone or facing a partner.

SANDY REE
SLAVE SONG FROM THE GEORGIA SEA ISLANDS

Way down yon - der,___ San - dy Ree,___ Where I come from,

San - dy Ree,___ Girls___ love boys,___ San - dy Ree,___ like a

hog loves corn, San - dy Ree.___ Oh,___ babe,_____

San - dy Ree,___ Oh,___ babe, San - dy Ree,___

Oh, babe,___ San - dy Ree,___ Oh,___ babe, San - dy Ree.___

2. Dog on the porch, . . .
   Kicking off fleas, . . .
   Chicken in the yard, . . .
   Scratching up peas, . . .

3. Your dog bark, . . .
   He don't see nothin', . . .
   My dog bark, . . .
   He done see somethin', . . .

📖 For other movement activities, see pp. 237–250.

Meter in 3

As you listen to the song, try these hand motions to match the meter in 3. Is the tempo fast, moderate, or slow?

SHRIMP BOATS

WORDS AND MUSIC BY PAUL HOWARD AND PAUL WESTON

Shrimp boats is a - com - in', their sails are in sight.

Shrimp boats is a - com - in', there's danc - in' to - night.

Why don't you hur - ry, hur - ry, hur - ry home?

Why don't you hur - ry, hur - ry, hur - ry home?

Shrimp boats is a - com - in', there's danc - in' to - night.

Show the rhythm of the words in phrases 1 and 2 and the last phrase by lightly clapping your left hand in the palm of your right hand.

During the two short phrases, show the rhythm of the words by clapping your right hand in the palm of your left hand.

Compare the two rhythm patterns.

Rhythm Patterns

As you listen to this song, find the rhythm patterns that repeat.

BIG ROCK CANDY MOUNTAIN

AMERICAN FOLK SONG

1. In the Big Rock Can - dy Moun-tain There's a land that's fair and bright,
2. In the Big Rock Can - dy Moun-tain All the cows have wood-en legs,

Where the hand-outs grow on bush - es, And you sleep out ev - 'ry night;
And the bull - dogs all are tooth-less, And the hens lay soft-boiled eggs,

Where the box - cars all are emp - ty, And the sun shines ev - 'ry day,
All the trees are full of ap - ples, And the barns are full of hay,

Oh, I'm bound to go where there is - n't an - y snow, Where the
There's a lake of stew and_____ so - da pop,_____ too, You can

rain does-n't fall and the wind does-n't blow, In the Big Rock Can - dy
paddle all a-round in a big ca - noe, In the Big Rock Can - dy

Moun - tain.
Moun - tain. Oh, the buzz-in' of the bees in the syc - a - more trees Round the

so - da wa - ter foun - tain, Where the lem - on - ade springs and the

blue - bird sings In the Big Rock Can - dy Moun - tain.

Rhythm Patterns

For a tambourine accompaniment, play one of these rhythm patterns throughout the song. The patterns taken from the song match the meter in 4, shown in line 1.

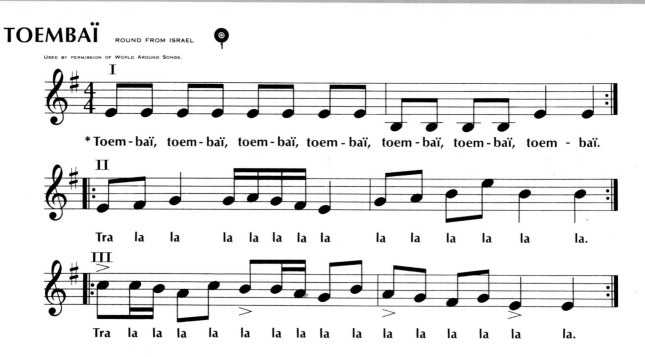

TOEMBAÏ   ROUND FROM ISRAEL

USED BY PERMISSION OF WORLD AROUND SONGS.

*Toem - baï, toem - baï, toem - baï, toem - baï, toem - baï, toem - baï, toem - baï.

Tra la la la la la la la la la la la la la.

Tra la la la la la la la la la la la la la la.

*pronounced to rhyme with *Poem-by*

Find the accents (>) in the third phrase. An accent is a sudden loudness. How will you play an accent on a tambourine?

Dividing the Steady Beat

This song from Canada has two sections, A and B. Which one
uses mostly eighth notes?

VIVE LA CANADIENNE! FOLK SONG FROM CANADA ENGLISH VERSION BY ROSEMARY JACQUES

1. Vi - ve la Ca - na - dien - ne! Vo - le, mon coeur,
1. Here's to the girl from Ca - na - da! How she makes my

vo - le! Vi - ve la Ca - na - dien - ne Et
poor___ heart___ beat! Here's to the girl from Ca - na - da With

ses jo - lis yeux doux, Et ses jo - lis yeux
eyes so___ ver - y sweet. Her pret - ty eyes are

doux, doux, doux, Et ses jo - lis yeux doux._____
ver - y sweet, Her eyes are ver - y sweet._____

2. On danse avec nos blondes,
   Vole, mon coeur, vole!
   On danse avec nos blondes;
   Nous changeons tour à tour,
   Nous changeons tour à tour, tour, tour,
   Nous changeons tour à tour.

2. *Someone is dancing with her now,*
   How she makes my poor heart beat!
   Someone is dancing with her now,
   But soon we two shall meet.
   But very soon we two shall meet,
   But soon we two shall meet.

Find the ways the steady beat
is divided in the rhythm patterns
in Section A.

For guitar fingerings, see p. 204.

Combining Groups of 2 and 3

Sometimes music from Greece uses a rhythm pattern combining groups of threes and groups of twos, making a meter of 7. Practice this pattern on a drum to play with the recording. The first note of each set of threes and twos is accented. The pattern of accents creates its own rhythm. Take turns playing either part to accompany the singing.

SAMIOTISSA   MUSIC BY D. A. VERGONI   ENGLISH WORDS BY STELLA PHREDOPOLOUS

MELODY COPYRIGHT 1950 BY MICHAEL GAETANOS. ATHENS

Sa - mio - tis - sa, Sa - mio - tis - sa, You will re-turn to Sa -

mos.___ Sa - mio - tis - sa, Sa - mio - tis - sa, Is-land of beau-ty and de-

light.___ You will come home a - gain to me, Sa-mio-tis - sa, There's

mu - sic in the sum-mer night. ___ You will come home a - gain to

me, Sa-mio - tis - sa, There's mu - sic in the sum-mer night.___

Rhythm pattern is used in music throughout the world. In India, a rhythm cycle, called a *tala,* decides the pattern.

The tala used to accompany this music has seven beats. Follow the tala played on a drum by clapping on the beats marked with an **X**.

📖 For more about tala, see p. 73.

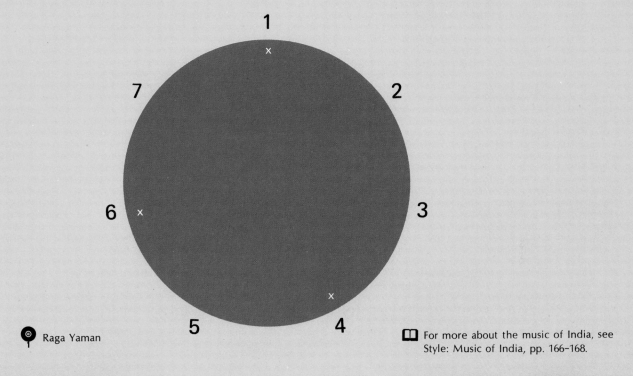

🔘 Raga Yaman

📖 For more about the music of India, see Style: Music of India, pp. 166–168.

SOUND PIECE 1   A Tic-Tac-Toe in Rhythm

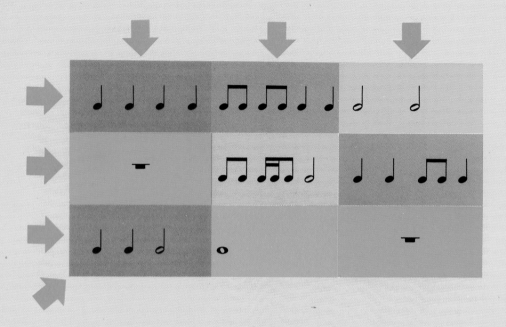

Tap or clap the patterns in any three boxes, one after the other,
by following any arrow. For silence, feel the beat without tapping.

To make the piece longer, follow more than one arrow.
Plan which arrows you will follow.

Add different tone colors by playing *Sound Piece 1* on a
percussion instrument, a recorder, a guitar—or an instrument you invent.

Sound Piece 1 can be played by one person or by several people,
starting together or a different times. All choose their own starting place.

Set a tempo before you begin. Will it be very fast, fast,
moderate, slow, or very slow?

Also choose a dynamic level for each part. Which part will be
soft? Which will be loud? Which will be moderate?

After playing *Sound Piece 1,* compose your own sound piece. Use any arrangement of boxes, any rhythm patterns, and any instruments. Here is an example.

Teach others to play your sound piece by explaining the idea, playing it for them, or helping them figure it out from your notation.

Treni: *Interlude*

CALL CHART 1: Rhythm Patterns

This call chart will help you hear some of the ways rhythm works in music. When a number is called, find that number on the call chart. Next to the number will be the word or words that describe what you are hearing.

1 STEADY BEAT—METER IN 2	6 STEADY BEAT—METER IN 3
2 CHANGE OF TEMPO	7 CHANGE OF TEMPO
3 STEADY BEAT	8 STEADY BEAT
4 CHANGE OF TEMPO	9 CHANGE OF TEMPO
5 STEADY BEAT	10 STEADY BEAT

How many things can you hear in this piece for flute and guitar?
Look at the list of qualities of music on p. 18 to help you.

🎵 Ibert: *Entr'acte*

In *Entr'acte* you heard and experienced sounds for their
own sake. No mind-pictures or stories or moods were
needed—just music alone. Such music is called
"absolute music."

This piece, *Symphonie fantastique,* is based on a story.
Sounds suggest and describe a series of events.
Such music is called *program music.*

Symphonie fantastique describes the dreams of a young
man in love. "March to the Scaffold," the fourth movement,
is a nightmare in which he is being led to his execution
for killing his loved one, a beautiful actress. Each time
she appears in his dreams, a haunting melody is played
by the clarinet.

🎵 Berlioz: *Symphonie fantastique,* "March to the Scaffold"

As you listen, choose as many words from p. 18 as you can
to describe what you hear.

Remember, in program music the story is just one part
of all the musical things to hear.

Sounds

BEAT strong beat / weak beat

TONALITY tonal center / major / minor

REGISTER mostly high / mostly low / both

MELODY Melody alone / melody with accompaniment

TEMPO very slow / slow / moderate / fast / very fast

PHRASES long phrases / short phrases / both long and short phrases

INTERVALS mostly steps / mostly leaps / mostly repeats / steps, leaps, and repeats

DURATION mostly long sounds / mostly short sounds / both long and short sounds

BEAT steady / getting faster / getting slower / stop and hold / no steady beat

DIRECTION mostly upward / mostly downward / both upward and downward

TONE COLOR— INSTRUMENTS flute / guitar / violin / bass / trumpet / drum

DYNAMICS loud / soft / getting louder / getting softer

TEXTURE melody alone / with harmony / with other melodies

TONE COLOR— VOICE man / woman / children / chorus

FORM A B / A B A / A B A C A

METER twos / threes

WHAT HAPPENS WHEN YOU LISTEN TO MUSIC?

MIND perceives
It sorts out what the sounds are doing and how they are related to each other.

Ears hear

FEELINGS react
You become involved by responding to what the sounds are doing.

Sounds + Ears + Mind + Feelings = Listening Experience

MORE ABOUT RHYTHM
Music with Two Meters

Notice how this song uses two meters. Section A is in $\frac{3}{4}$. What is the meter of Section B?

MINEIRA DE MINAS

COMPOSER UNKNOWN   ENGLISH WORDS BY ROSEMARY JACQUES

For guitar fingerings, see p. 204.

For percussion parts, see pp. 224 and 225.

Music with Three Meters

This song uses a pattern of three different meters.

The first measure uses $\frac{2}{4}$. Name the other two meters.

Clap or tap the beats as you sing the song.

LOOK OUT!   WORDS AND MUSIC BY DORIS HAYS

© 1973 DORIS HAYS

Look out! Off the ground, turn a - round, what's that sound?

It's that rock - et roar - ing in the sky, just a speck in my eye,

Won - der if they're fly - ing to the moon, or to Mars, or Nep-tune,

Or some dis - tant star So ver - y far that we are like - ly to

run right out of breath!

How many times does this pattern appear?

Are these two rhythm patterns the same, or different?

For percussion parts, see p. 226.

Rhythm Patterns in 2 Meter

As you listen to the recording, play a tambourine on each beat.

This will help you feel the change in tempo as the song is repeated.

HALLELUJAH FOLK SONG FROM ISRAEL

FROM GOOD TIMES SONG BOOK BY JAMES F. LEISY, PUBLISHED BY ABINGDON PRESS.

Hal - le - lu - jah, hal - le - lu - jah, hal - le - lu - jah, hal - le - lu!

Hal - le - lu - jah, hal - le - lu - jah, hal - le - lu - jah, hal - le - lu!

Hal - le - lu - jah, hal - le - lu, hal - le - lu - jah, hal - le - lu!

Hal - le - lu - jah, hal - le - lu - jah, hal - le - lu - jah, hal - le - lu!

Play one of these rhythm patterns on the tambourine throughout the song.

Notice that the beat shown by a quarter note (♩) can be divided

into two sounds (♫), called eighth notes.

Rhythm Patterns in 3 Meter

How many different rhythm patterns can you find in this song
in three meter?

EL CAPOTIN   FOLK SONG FROM PUERTO RICO

Try playing recorder or bells to accompany Section B. Improvise
(make up) your own rhythm pattern on the pitch A.

Try singing Section B in two parts.

Syncopation

Listen to the recording to hear how beats are organized to create a special feeling called *syncopation*.

I'M GONNA SING OUT
WORDS AND MUSIC BY DAVID EDDLEMAN

Clap the rhythm pattern ♫♫♪ each time it comes in the song. How many times does it appear?

Try singing a harmony part for "I'm Gonna Sing Out." It uses many repeated tones as well as syncopation. Some arrangements of long and short sounds are the same as the melody; some are different.

Lord, my Lord, _____ I'm gon - na sing out, ___

____ my Lord, _____ I'm gon - na sing out, ___

____ my Lord, ___ I'm gon - na sing out, ___ sing out,

Gon - na sing 'til the Judg - ment Day.

Add a syncopated pattern as you listen to the ensemble.

Play a tambourine, small drum, or triangle.

For more about syncopation, see p. 234.

Syncopation

Play one of these percussion parts to accompany this song.

Notice how quarter and eighth notes are used in $\frac{4}{4}$ meter.

THANK YOU FOR THE CHRIS'MUS
FOLK SONG FROM JAMAICA

COLLECTED AND TRANSCRIBED BY OLIVE LEWIN   REPRINTED BY PERMISSION OF MISS OLIVE LEWIN AND THE ORGANIZATION OF AMERICAN STATES.

Thank you for ____ the Chris'-mus, Thank you for ____ the

New Year, And thank you for ____ the chance to live ____ to

see an-oth-er Chris'-mus / New Year La la la la, Do-in' the

bam-boo walk, ____ La la la la, Do-in' the bam-boo walk. ____

Now play a phrase that uses syncopation.

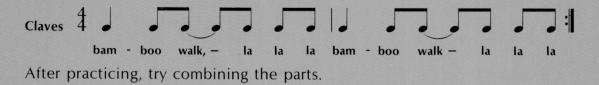

bam - boo walk, — la la la bam - boo walk — la la la

After practicing, try combining the parts.

Is the song in major, or minor, tonality?

Hearing Rhythm Patterns

Listen for the rhythm pattern made by the words of this song.

Do you hear long sounds, short sounds, or both?

Do you hear syncopation?

PAT-A-PAN   EARLY BURGUNDIAN FRENCH CAROL   ENGLISH WORDS BY ROSEMARY JACQUES

1. Wil - lie, bring your fin - est drum; Rob-in, take your flute and

come; Play a joy - ful song of praise, *Tu-re-lu-re-lu,* *pat-a-pat-a-*

pan, Play a joy - ful song of praise On this won-drous day of days.

2. Long ago on Christmas morn
   When the holy Child was born,
   Shepherds from the fields did come,
   Turelurelu, patapatapan,
   Shepherds from the fields did come
   Playing on their pipe and drum.

3. So 'tis fitting on this day
   That on instruments we play,
   Like the humble shepherd men,
   Turelurelu, patapatapan,
   Like the humble shepherd men
   Who were there in Bethlehem.

Practice one of these parts to accompany the singing of "Pat-a-Pan."

Recorder or Bells

Is the song in major, or minor, tonality?

For rhythm parts, see p. 227.

STYLE: RESPONDING TO AFRICAN MUSIC

This song is part of a story told by the Shona people of Rhodesia. The story is about Karingano, a beautiful girl whose mother keeps her in a cave to protect her from young men. So that food can be brought to her, Karingano is told to come out of the cave only when she hears her mother singing.

The audience joins the storyteller in singing *Mai Wakaringano,* which means "Mother of Karingano."

As you listen to the song, respond to the story just as the Shona people do, by singing the response.

 Mai Wakaringano

If you were a young person growing up in Africa, you might learn music by listening rather than by reading notation. You might respond to stories like the story of Karingano, or you might make work less tiresome by learning to sing a song.

In this grinding song, two women are complaining about Debura's lazy husband while they grind grain between rocks to make flour.

Debura

The leader's part is the *call*. The answering, or lower, part is the *response*. The call-and-response form has influenced many styles of music, including spirituals, jazz, and rock.

Take turns singing the call and the response parts and playing the rhythm of the grinding.

Sometimes people in Shona society dance to the sounds of rattles and various-sized drums.

Listen for the rhythm pattern played on the rattle throughout this dance music.

🎵 2 Kalanga Dance

1 2 3 4 5 6 7 8 9 10 11 12

When you listen again, hear the drums play different rhythms above this basic pattern. One of the drums is being rubbed with a stick. The others are struck.

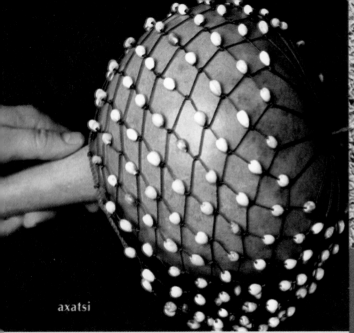

axatsi

gankogui

conga drum

The mbira (kalimba) is the most important instrument of the Shona people. It is played as a solo instrument for recreation, as well as in an ensemble for rituals.

There are many types of mbira in Africa, with different arrangements of keys and different playing styles. Sometimes the player will give a special name to his mbira and will sing in response to it in the same way he would respond to a person singing a call.

Listen to the tone color of the mbira.

 Hande Hande

2

Shona music often has many voice parts that fit with each other in the same way that drum patterns in a dance ensemble are related.

Here is a song, originally sung at a time of great famine, that has four voice parts. Try to hear the four separate parts and how they weave together. The notation shows what each group is singing.

Notice how the parts are written in different clefs, treble and bass. What is the relationship between the register (high or low) of the voices and the clef used in the notation?

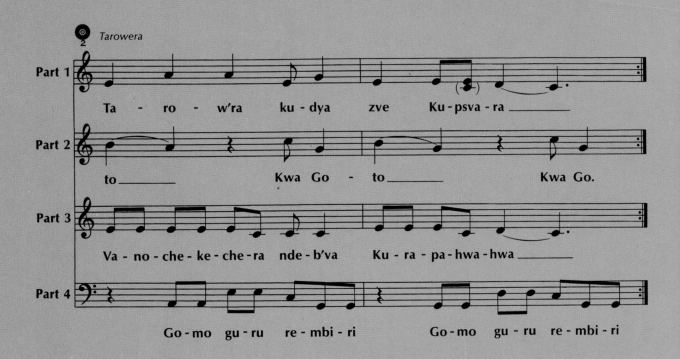

Tarowera

Part 1: Ta - ro - w'ra   ku - dya   zve   Ku - psva - ra _____

Part 2: to _____   Kwa Go - to _____   Kwa Go.

Part 3: Va - no - che - ke - che - ra   nde - b'va   Ku - ra - pa - hwa - hwa _____

Part 4: Go - mo   gu - ru   re - mbi - ri   Go - mo   gu - ru   re - mbi - ri

Practice the rhythm pattern on which each part is based.
Play the drum on the counts shown by the enlarged numbers.

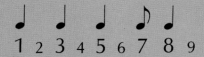

1 2 **3** 4 **5** 6 **7** 8 **9**

Polyrhythm in African Music

Count each line of the following set of numbers. Clap on the enlarged numbers only.

1. **1** 2 **3** 4 **5 6** 7 **8** 9 **10** 11 **12**

2. **1** 2 3 **4** 5 6 **7** 8 9 **10** 11 12

3. **1** 2 **3 4 5 6 7 8 9 10 11 12**

4. **1 2 3 4** 5 6 **7 8 9 10** 11 12

5. 1 2 **3 4** 5 **6 7** 8 **9 10** 11 12

🔊 African Rhythm Complex
2

Choose one line to play over and over as others in the class clap different lines. You hear a combination of rhythm patterns called *polyrhythm*.

These rhythm lines can be played on instruments. Look at the notation for the rhythms you clapped. Practice your part so you hear polyrhythm with a combination of tone colors.

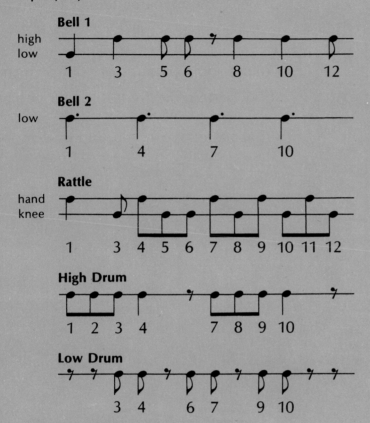

Bell 1

high
low

1   3   5 6   8   10   12

Bell 2

low

1   4   7   10

Rattle

hand
knee

1   3 4 5 6   7 8 9   10 11 12

High Drum

1 2 3 4   7 8 9 10

Low Drum

3 4   6 7   9 10

EXPERIENCING THE ARTS: PATTERN
Introducing Pattern

Patterns can be made by lines, shapes, colors. How many patterns can you find in these photographs?

Collect some pictures of your own that show patterns of things in your community.

What patterns can you find in this poem?

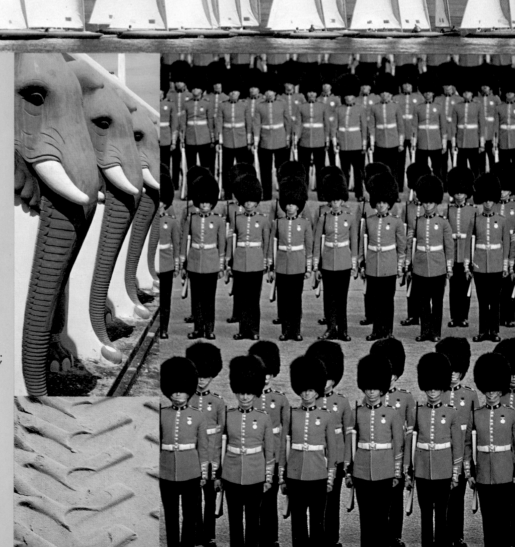

SUMMER GRASS

Summer grass aches
   and whispers.

It wants something;
it calls out and sings;
it pours out wishes
   to the overhead stars.

The rain hears;
the rain answers;
the rain is slow coming;
the rain wets the face
   of the grass.

Carl Sandburg

In "Summer Grass" you can see and hear pattern. The word "it" at the beginning of some lines forms a pattern. What other words form a pattern?

 Sandburg: Summer Grass

What is the pattern of punctuation in the poem?

What is the pattern formed by the length of lines?

Both poetry and music use pattern.

Notice the rhythm pattern that is repeated in every measure of this song.

As you sing the song, find the patterns that are alike in both rhythm and melody.

EMMA

FOLK SONG FROM TRINIDAD AND TOBAGO

USED BY PERMISSION OF DR. J. D. ELDER, PH.D (PENN. UNIV.), ANTHROPOLOGIST, CHAIRMAN, NATIONAL CULTURAL COUNCIL OF TRINIDAD AND TOBAGO, WEST INDIES.

Em - ma, le' me 'lone, le' me 'lone. Me no mar - ry yet, le' me 'lone.

Em - ma, le' me 'lone, le' me 'lone. Me no mar - ry yet, le' me 'lone.

When me mar - ry, oh, bell go ring. When me mar - ry, oh, shell go blow.

Em - ma, le' me 'lone, le' me 'lone. Me no mar - ry yet, le' me 'lone.

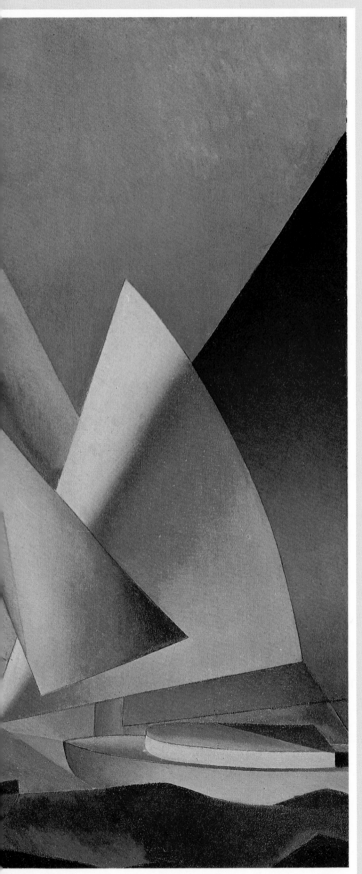

SHEELER, CHARLES: PERTAINING TO YACHTS AND YACHTING. PHILADELPHIA MUSEUM OF ART: BEQUEST OF MARGARETTA S. HINCHMAN '55-96-9.

You have seen pattern in photographs
of familiar objects, in poetry,
in a song, and in a painting.
Now hear how pattern is used
in this piece for orchestra.

Listen for the repeated rhythm
pattern and tap it lightly.

Stravinsky: *Agon*, "Bransle Gay"

We see pattern in painting.

We hear pattern in music.

Experiencing the Arts: Pattern 37

Now find repeated rhythm patterns in *The Star-Spangled Banner.*

THE STAR-SPANGLED BANNER

MUSIC BY JOHN STAFFORD SMITH

WORDS BY FRANCIS SCOTT KEY

PHRASE 1

1. Oh,___ say! can you see, by the dawn's ear - ly light, What so
2. On the shore, dim - ly seen through the mists of the deep, Where the
3. Oh,___ thus be it ever when___ free men shall stand Be -

PHRASE 2

proud - ly we hailed at the twi - light's last gleam - ing, Whose broad
foe's haugh - ty host in dread si - lence re - pos - es, What is
tween their loved homes and the war's des - o - la - tion! Blest with

PHRASE 3

stripes and bright stars, through the per - il - ous fight, O'er the
that which the breeze, o'er the tow - er - ing steep, As it
vic - t'ry and peace, may the heav'n - res - cued land Praise the

PHRASE 4

ram - parts we watched were so gal - lant - ly stream - ing? And the
fit - ful - ly blows, half con - ceals, half dis - clos - es? Now it
Pow'r that hath made and pre - served us a na - tion! Then___

Patterns in Movement

All the arts use pattern in their own way. In dance the movement of the body creates patterns.

As you listen to this music, clap this rhythm. Listen for the steady beat before starting to clap.

🎵 *Yes Me Siroon*
2

Now show the same pattern with your feet. Join hands and walk in a circle.

right   left   right   left   right   left

Still holding hands, face the center of the circle and move sideways to the right.

step right   cross left in back   step right   cross left in front

cross right over left   step left   right in back of left   step left

After practicing, dance the pattern with a group, moving in a circle.

Your movement in a circle created another kind of pattern, called a *floor pattern*.

📖 For other movement activities, see pp. 237–250.

40 Experiencing the Arts: Pattern

WHAT DO YOU HEAR? 1: Rhythm Patterns

Point to the notation in each box that shows
the rhythm pattern you hear.

1.

2.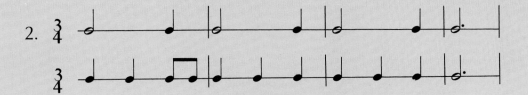

3.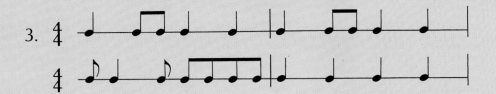

4.

5.

6.

SECTION 2
INTRODUCTION TO FORM

Sounds are not music until they are organized in some way.
The organization of a piece of music—the way it is put together—is
its form. In this section you will learn some more about
the forms of music.

Form is all around us. Our lives would be confused and bewildering
if we did not organize things. We need to give form to our world.

What gives a sense of order—form—to these things?
Use such words in your discussion as:

patterns	variations	balance and imbalance
contrast	repetition	expected and unexpected

USING WHAT YOU KNOW ABOUT FORM
Repetition and Contrast of Sections

Most songs are "put together" with sections that repeat and sections that contrast. Listen to the sections that repeat and contrast in this song. The letters A and B in the score will help you hear the beginning and ending of sections.

LAZYBONES

WORDS AND MUSIC BY JOHNNY MERCER AND HOAGY CARMICHAEL

COPYRIGHT 1933 BY SOUTHERN MUSIC PUBLISHING CO. INC. COPYRIGHT RENEWED. USED BY PERMISSION.

La - zy - bones, sleep-in' in the sun, How you 'spec' to get your day's work done? Nev - er get your day's work done, Sleep - in' in the noon - day sun. La - zy - bones, sleep - in' in the shade, How you 'spec' to get your corn - meal made? Nev-er get your corn-meal made, Sleep-in' in the eve - nin' shade.

In Section A, think of four natural sounds to play on each of the four beats in each measure: snap fingers, tap foot, tap windowpane, scrape window blind, etc.

In Section B, make four different motions, one for each of the four beats in each measure: shrug shoulders, wave right hand, wave left hand, etc.

Repetition and Contrast of Sections

Follow the diagram as you listen to this song to hear which section repeats and which section is a contrast.

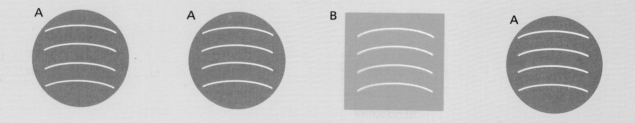

MOUNTAIN SOUND

© 1972 DAVID McHUGH

WORDS AND MUSIC BY DAVID McHUGH

1. When the sky is clear at sun - down,
2. Hear the owl a - soft - ly call - in',
4. Wake up ear - ly with the sun - rise,

And the stars start a - com - in'_____ round,_____
Hear the bob - cat_____ in the_____ tree,_____
Nev - er could when I lived in_____ town,_____

Look out yon - der to the moun - tain,
While the night is soft - ly fall - in',
But I nev - er had the peace of mind

Fine

Lis - ten to that moun - tain sound.
Moun - tain sound is call - in' me.
Of liv - ing with that moun - tain sound.

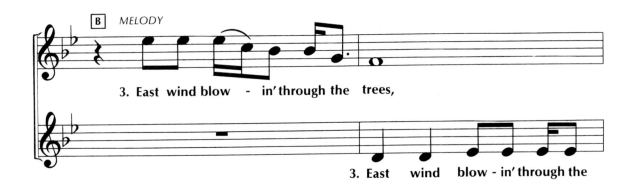

3. East wind blow - in' through the trees,

3. East wind blow - in' through the

Moon-light danc - in' on the leaves,

trees, Moon - light danc - in' on the

Cit - y's gone _____ and my mind's at _____ ease, And I

leaves, And my mind's at ease, And I'll

D.C. al Fine

feel as if I'll nev - er want to leave.

nev - er want to leave.

Music with Two Sections

This song is put together in two sections, A and B.

Which section ends upward?

Which section ends downward?

IT'S A SMALL WORLD

WORDS AND MUSIC BY RICHARD M. SHERMAN AND ROBERT B. SHERMAN

© 1963 WONDERLAND MUSIC CO., INC. REPRINTED BY PERMISSION

1. It's a world of laugh - ter, a world of tears;
2. There is just one moon and one gold - en sun,

It's a world of hopes and a world of fears.
And a smile means friend - ship to ev - 'ry - one.

There's so much that we share that it's time we're a - ware,
Though the moun - tains di - vide and the o - ceans are wide,

It's a small world af - ter all. _____

Each section has a different melody, but these contrasting sections can be sung at the same time.

It's a small world af - ter all,

It's a small world af - ter all,

It's a small world af - ter all,

It's a small, small world. _____

WHAT DO YOU HEAR? 2: Form

These pieces have two sections. The form is AB.

Choose the word or words that tell how the sections contrast.

1.	MAJOR-MINOR	METER
2.	RHYTHM	METER
3.	TONE COLOR	MAJOR-MINOR
4.	MELODY	METER
5.	MAJOR-MINOR	METER

Music with Three Sections

This song has three sections, A B C
Listen to the recording of this song and choose one
of the sections to accompany with Autoharp or percussion
instruments. See the suggested percussion parts on p. 51.

TZENA, TZENA

FOLK SONG FROM ISRAEL   ENGLISH WORDS BY PHYLLIS RESNICK

Tze - na, tze - na, tze - na, tze - na, come in - to the fields and we'll be -
gin _____ to work the land. Hoe - ing, sow - ing, new things grow - ing,
pi - o - neer - ing all to - geth - er, come _____ and lend a hand.
Tze - na, tze - na, build - ing a new na - tion,
toil - ing bus - i - ly all day. _____ Soon we'll dance and

50 Using . . . Form

have a cel - e - bra - tion, But first we'll work and then we'll play.

Tze - na, tze - na, (clap) Tze - na, tze - na, tze - na, Tze - na, tze - na,

Tze - na, tze - na, tze - na, tze - na, Tze - na, tze - na,

(clap) Tze - na, tze - na, tze - na, Tze - na, tze - na, Tze - na, tze - na, tze - na.

Woodblock

A

Handclap

B

Tambourine

C

shake   strike

📖 For a percussion ensemble, see p. 228.

📖 For directions for dancing the hora, see p. 243.

Rondo Form

A *rondo* is a special arrangement of contrasting sections. Can you discover the arrangement of this rondo by looking at the photographs on page 53.

Listen to become familiar with Section A before following the Call Chart.

CALL CHART 2: Rondo   Mouret: *Symphonie de fanfares,* "Rondeau"

1	SECTION A	TRUMPET SOLO; FOUR PHRASES— PHRASES 1 AND 3 ARE EXACTLY ALIKE, PHRASES 2 AND 4 ARE NEARLY ALIKE.
2	SECTION B	NO TRUMPET; TWO PHRASES, ALIKE IN RHYTHM AND MELODY
3	SECTION A	PHRASES 3 AND 4 ONLY
4	SECTION C	NO TRUMPET; LONG AND SHORT PHRASES
5	SECTION A	SAME AS NUMBER 1

As this piece moves along, you hear how contrast in music can be created in many ways.

- changes in rhythm pattern
- changes in melody
- changes in tone color
- changes in dynamics

Repetition and contrast is organized in this piece in a special form called *rondo*—A B A C A.

Repetition and Contrast of Sections—Dance

You have played, sung, and listened to music that is "put together" in three sections. Listen to the recording of *Tarantella*, a folk dance tune from Italy, to hear three contrasting sections.

 Tarantella

The movements in the folk dance show the contrast between the sections.

DANCE

Partners stand side by side in a set of 8, as shown in the diagram.

SECTION A

Keeping the same places in the set, all run forward around the room and back to place. Try to get back to place when the repeat of Section A comes to an end (16 measures in all).

SECTION B

Partners face each other in the set.

Phrase 1 (2 measures): All run forward four steps, passing right shoulders with partner.

Phrase 2 (2 measures): All take four running steps in place, turning around to face partner.

Phrase 3: same as phrase 1.

Phrase 4: same as phrase 2.

SECTION C

Partners still facing, hands on hips.

Phrase 1 (4 measures): While hopping on left foot, point right toe to front, then to the side—front, side, front, side, throughout the phrase.

Phrase 2 (4 measures): Join hands and change places in set.

SECTION C REPEATED

Phrase 1 (4 measures): Same as phrase 1, but hop on right foot.

Phrase 2 (4 measures): Join hands and return to place.

Add your own piano part during the contrasting section
on the recording used in the Call Chart.

Choose one of the patterns below to play in any register
of the piano—high, middle, or low.

Play each note of the pattern you choose eight times, using the
index finger of either hand.

Be ready to play the pattern over as many times as you hear it
on the recording in the contrasting section.

Any number can play.

Can you hear the tones of the four patterns sounded together,
creating *harmony*?

The horizontal and vertical lines show what you hear.

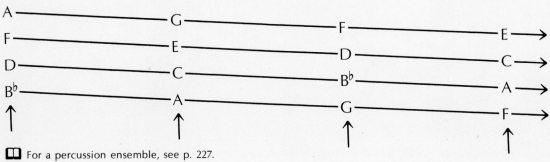

📖 For a percussion ensemble, see p. 227.
📖 For a stone-passing game, see p. 239.

EXPERIENCING THE ARTS: FORM

Can you name some of the parts of a bicycle? Of a car?
Of a motorcycle?

All the parts work together to make the whole bicycle, car, or
motorcycle. Each part adds something important.

The arts are made of parts that work together.

COMPOSITION WITH CLARINETS AND TIN HORN BY BEN SHAHN, AMERICAN 1898–1969.
COLLECTION OF THE DETROIT INSTITUTE OF ARTS. GIFT OF THE FRIENDS OF MODERN ART.

Some of the same parts—things you can see—are used in these
two paintings. Can you find them?

• a foreground (in front) and a background
• darker colors against lighter colors
• strong vertical (up and down) shapes
• strong horizontal (side to side) shapes or lines across the bottom
and across the middle
• a round, white, active shape in the same position in each painting
• a large rounded yellow shape in the same position in each painting

The two paintings
have a similar form
(arrangement of
parts), yet each
has its own
special look.

MARISOL: THE FAMILY. COLLECTION, THE MUSEUM OF MODERN ART, NEW YORK, ADVISORY COMMITTEE FUND.

In poetry, some of the parts that make up the whole are images (mind-pictures), rhymes (although not every poem uses rhyme), length of lines, and rhythm of the words.

Look for these things in this poem:

- words that give you images
- rhyme
- arrangement of long and short lines
- the rhythm—flow—of the words

FOURTH OF JULY NIGHT

The little boat at anchor
in black water sat murmuring
to the tall black sky.

   * * *

 A white sky bomb fizzed on a black line.
 A rocket hissed its red signature into the west.
 Now a shower of Chinese fire alphabets,
 a cry of flower pots broken in flames,
 a long curve to a purple spray,
 three violet balloons—

  Drips of seaweed tangled in gold,
  shimmering symbols of mixed numbers,
  tremulous arrangements of cream gold folds
  of a bride's wedding gown—

   * * *

A few sky bombs spoke their pieces,
then velvet dark.

The little boat at anchor
in black water sat murmuring
to the tall black sky.

Carl Sandburg

In music, the parts that work together to form a whole are sounds.
Sounds can get louder or softer. They can go slower or faster.
They can change tone color and density, get higher and lower,
repeat and contrast.

How many of these parts can you hear working together as you listen?
The chart below will help you identify the parts within a whole piece.

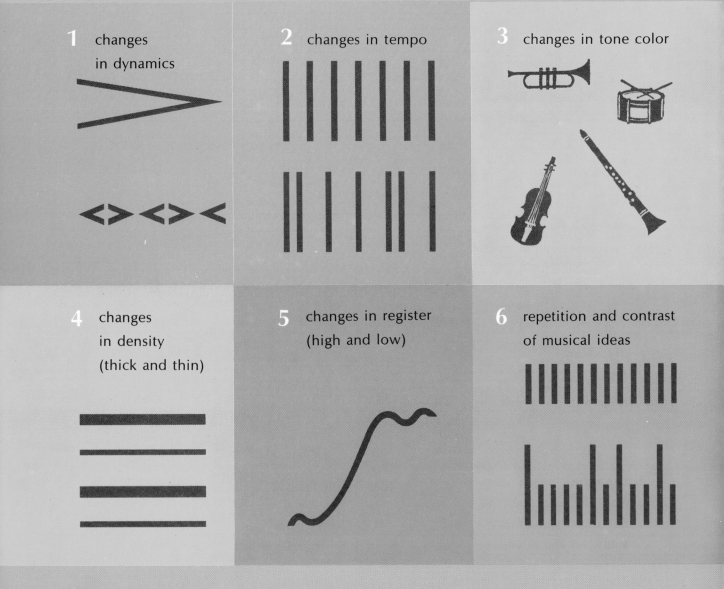

1 changes in dynamics

2 changes in tempo

3 changes in tone color

4 changes in density (thick and thin)

5 changes in register (high and low)

6 repetition and contrast of musical ideas

Stravinsky: *Rite of Spring,* "Evocation of Ancestors" and "Ritual of Ancestors"

In every art, the whole is formed from parts working together.
We notice the parts, but we also experience the work as a whole.

MORE ABOUT FORM
Repetition and Contrast of Phrases

A phrase is a musical thought. As you sing this song, feel the length of each phrase.

Which phrases are alike? Which phrases are different?

ON TOP OF OLD SMOKY   FOLK SONG FROM KENTUCKY

1. On top of old Smok - y,_____
2. A - court - in's a pleas - ure,_____

All cov - ered with snow,_____
A - flirt - in's a grief,_____

I lost my true lov - er,_____
A false - heart - ed lov - er_____

A - court - in' too slow._____
Is_____ worse than a thief._____

3. For a thief, he will rob you
   And take what you have,
   But a falsehearted lover
   Will send you to your grave.

4. They'll hug you and kiss you,
   And tell you more lies
   Than the crossties on the railroad,
   Or the stars in the skies.

5. Come, all you young maidens,
   And listen to me,
   Never place your affections
   On a green willow tree.

6. The leaves they will wither,
   The roots they will die,
   You'll all be forsaken,
   And never know why.

For recorder parts, see p. 209.

As you sing this song, look at the notation. Which phrase has more repeated tones at the beginning?

HE'S GOT THE WHOLE WORLD IN HIS HANDS

BLACK SPIRITUAL

1. He's got the whole world ____ in his hands, ____
2. He's got the wind and rain ____ in his hands, ____
3. He's got both you and me ____ in his hands, ____

He's got the whole world ____ in his hands, ____
He's got the wind and rain ____ in his hands, ____
He's got both you and me ____ in his hands, ____

He's got the whole world ____ in his hands, ____
He's got the wind and rain ____ in his hands, ____
He's got both you and me ____ in his hands, ____

He's got the whole world in his hands. _____
He's got the whole world in his hands. _____
He's got the whole world in his hands. _____

Can you tell what the diagram shows?

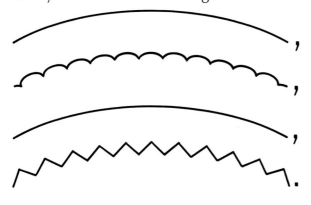

For a guitar part in the key of C, see p. 193.

More About Form 65

Repetition and Contrast of Phrases

DEEP BLUE SEA   AMERICAN FOLK SONG

phrase 1

1. Deep   blue   sea,   ba - by,   deep   blue   sea,

phrase 2

Deep   blue   sea,   ba - by,   deep   blue   sea,

phrase 3

Deep   blue   sea,   ba - by,   deep   blue   sea,

phrase 4

It   was   Wil - lie_____   what   got   drown - ded

In   the   deep   blue   sea.

2. Low'r him down with a
   golden chain, (*3 times*)
   It was Willie . . .

3. Dig his grave with a
   silver spade, (*3 times*)

4. Wrap him up in a silken
   shroud, (*3 times*)

5. Golden sun bring him back to me, (*3 times*)

Which of these phrases have the same rhythm?

Which have the same melody?

How is phrase 4 a contrast?

Take turns playing an Autoharp accompaniment. In which
phrases do you find repetition in the order of chords?

In which phrases is there a contrast?

For a drum part, see p. 230.

This piece, composed about 600 years ago, uses a phrase structure of repetitions and contrasts. The chart will help you hear how the phrases create the form.

At call number 1, Introduction, there are drum beats and a trombone "call" of a few notes. The call is shown by 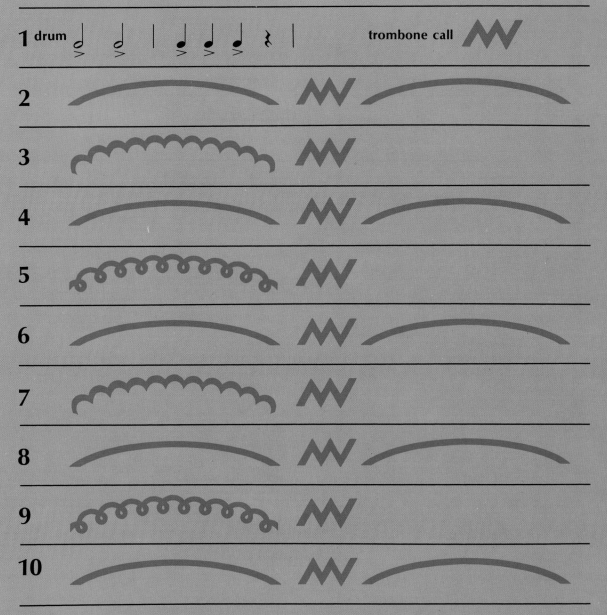 on the chart. Notice how the call connects phrases throughout the piece.

Anonymous: *Trotto*

CALL CHART 4: Form

Phrases and Sections

Add a handclapping pattern to each section of this song.

THANK GOD, I'M A COUNTRY BOY

WORDS AND MUSIC BY JOHN MARTIN SOMMERS

1. Well, life on a farm is kind-a laid back, ain't
2. When the work's all___ done and the sun's___ settin' low I

much an old coun-try boy like me can't hack. It's
pull___ out my fid-dle and I ro-sin up my bow. But the

ear-ly to rise, ear-ly in the sack; Thank
kids___ are a-sleep so I keep it kind-a low; Thank

God, I'm a coun-try boy.___ A sim-ple kind-a life nev-er
God, I'm a coun-try boy.___ I'd play "Sal-ly Goodin'" all___

did me no harm, Rais-in' me a fam-i-ly and
day if I could, but the Lord and my wife___ would-n't

work-in' on a farm. My days are all filled with an
take it ver-y good. So I fid-dle when I can and I

eas-y coun-try charm; Thank God, I'm a coun-try boy.___
work___ when I should; Thank God, I'm a coun-try boy.___

B REFRAIN

Well, I got me a fine wife, I got me old fid-dle. When the

sun's com-in' up I got cakes___ on the grid-dle; And

life ain't no-thin' but a fun-ny, fun-ny rid-dle; Thank

God, I'm a coun-try boy.___

3. I wouldn't trade my life for diamonds or jewels,
I never was one of them money hungry fools.
I'd rather have my fiddle and my farmin' tools;
Thank God, I'm a country boy.
Yeah, city folk drivin' in a black limousine,
A lotta sad people thinkin' that's mighty keen.
Well, folks, let me tell you now exactly what I mean;
Thank God, I'm a country boy. *Refrain*

The dance follows the form of the song. The movement will show
Section A and Section B and how phrases in each section are organized.

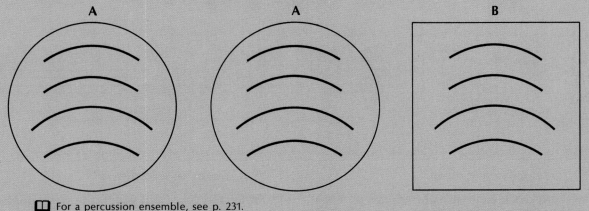

📖 For a percussion ensemble, see p. 231.
📖 For another square dance, see p. 247.

Phrase Endings— Cadences

Think of some special days and special events that you look forward to. You expect something to happen. This feeling of expectation is created in music, too.

As you sing this song, notice that the first three phrases in each section seem unfinished, or incomplete—something more is needed to complete the musical thought. The last phrase of each section seems finished, or complete.

The ending of a phrase is called a *cadence*.

For a guitar part, see p. 192.

For recorder parts, see pp. 210 and 211.

PAY ME MY MONEY DOWN

TRO—⊕ COPYRIGHT 1942 AND RENEWED 1970 HOLLIS MUSIC, INC. NEW YORK, N.Y. USED BY PERMISSION.

SLAVE SONG FROM THE GEORGIA SEA ISLANDS COLLECTED AND ADAPTED BY LYDIA A. PARRISH

1. I thought I heard the cap - tain say,
"Pay me my mon - ey down,—
To - mor - row is our sail - ing day,—
Pay me my mon - ey down."—

REFRAIN
"Pay me, oh, pay me,
Pay me my mon - ey down,—
Pay me or go to jail,—
Pay me my mon - ey down."—

2. As soon as the boat was clear of the bar,
   "Pay me my money down,"
   He knocked me down with the end of a spar,
   "Pay me my money down." *Refrain*

3. Well, I wish I was Mr. Steven's son,
   "Pay me my money down,"
   Sit on the bank and watch the work done,
   "Pay me my money down." *Refrain*

As in "Pay Me My Money Down," the first three phrases of this song seem unfinished, or incomplete. A sense of expectation continues throughout the song until the final tone.

STREETS OF LAREDO

AMERICAN COWBOY SONG

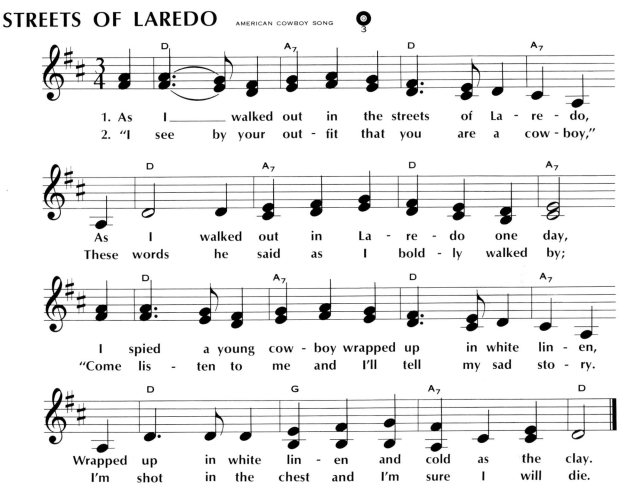

1. As I _____ walked out in the streets of La - re - do,
2. "I see by your out - fit that you are a cow - boy,"

As I walked out in La - re - do one day,
These words he said as I bold - ly walked by;

I spied a young cow - boy wrapped up in white lin - en,
"Come lis - ten to me and I'll tell my sad sto - ry.

Wrapped up in white lin - en and cold as the clay.
I'm shot in the chest and I'm sure I will die.

3. "Now once in the saddle I used to ride handsome,
   'A handsome young cowboy' is what they would say.
   I'd ride into town and go down to the card-house,
   But I'm shot in the chest and I'm dying today.

4. "Go run to the spring for a cup of cold water
   To cool down my fever," the young cowboy said.
   But when I returned, his poor soul had departed,
   And I wept when I saw the young cowboy was dead.

5. We'll bang the drum slowly and play the fife lowly,
   We'll play the dead march as we bear him along.
   We'll go to the graveyard and lay the sod o'er him;
   He was a young cowboy, but he had done wrong.

For guitar parts, see p. 194.

Anticipation and Expectation

Pachelbel: *Canon in D Major*

In this music, you will hear the lowest part, called a *ground bass,* repeat over and over throughout the piece. Follow the part in the circle to feel the sense of anticipation and expectation as the tones lead away from and back to the tonal center—the "home" tone.

Play one of the parts below on recorder, bells, or keyboard throughout the recording. Which one can you play? Practice so the parts can be played together.

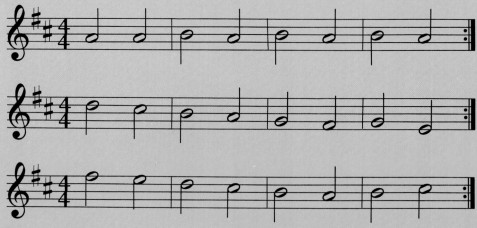

Now listen to a rock composition. The sense of anticipation and expectation is created by the pattern of chords. Follow the chords as they lead from one to another until the home chord is reached.

Striano, Luccisano, Gentile:
There's a Moon Out Tonight

D   B MIN.   G   A₇

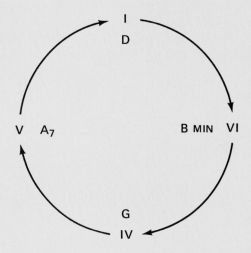

I
D

V   A₇   B MIN   VI

G
IV

In this music, a sense of expectation is created by the *tala,* or rhythm pattern. It uses a cycle of 7 beats described on p. 13.

Raga Maru-Bihag

More About Form   73

WHAT DO YOU HEAR? 3: Phrases ⊚₄

I. Listen for phrases that repeat or that contrast. At numbers 3, 4, 5, and 6 decide whether the phrase is a repeat of what you heard at number 2 (Phrase A) or is a contrasting phrase, B.

1	INTRODUCTION	
2	PHRASE A	
3	PHRASE A REPEATED	CONTRASTING PHRASE B
4	PHRASE A REPEATED	CONTRASTING PHRASE B
5	PHRASE A REPEATED	CONTRASTING PHRASE B
6	PHRASE A REPEATED	CONTRASTING PHRASE B

Anonymous: *Trotto*

II. How many phrases do you hear in this music? Choose the correct number for each piece.

1	1	2	3	4	5	Bach: *Cantata 79,* "Chorale" (excerpt)
2	1	2	3	4	5	Barber: *Adagio for Strings* (excerpt)
3	1	2	3	4	5	Polka (excerpt)
4	1	2	3	4	5	Hallelujah (excerpt)

III. When you hear a number called, decide whether it comes in the middle of a phrase or at the end of a phrase. Choose the correct answer.

1	MIDDLE	END
2	MIDDLE	END
3	MIDDLE	END
4	MIDDLE	END
5	MIDDLE	END
6	MIDDLE	END

Haydn: *Divertimento,* Movement 3

Cadences

Listen to the phrases of this song. Which end with a weak cadence?

Which phrases end with a strong cadence?

THANKSGIVING CHORALE

MUSIC BY J. L. STEINER   WORDS BY JOHN ARLOTT

"GOD'S FARM" BY JOHN ARLOTT. REPRINTED BY PERMISSION OF JOHN ARLOTT

1. God, whose farm___ is all cre - a - tion,

Take the grat - i - tude we give;

Take the fin - est of our har - vest,

Crops___ we___ grow that___ men may live.

2. Take our ploughing, seeding, reaping,
   Hopes and fears of sun and rain,
   All our thinking, planning, waiting,
   Ripened in this fruit and grain.

3. All our labor, all our watching,
   All our calendar of care,
   In these crops of your creation,
   Take, O God: they are our prayer.

If you can play low D, G, A, B, C, high D, and high E on the recorder, try playing the melody.

If you are a beginner on the recorder, try playing the countermelody.

Recorder or bells

Repetition and Contrast of Phrases and Sections

Sounds are not music until they are organized in some way—given a form. The form of this song is shown in the diagram.
Follow the phrases as you listen to each section.

A   A   B   A

WINTER WONDERLAND

MUSIC BY FELIX BERNARD   WORDS BY DICK SMITH

© 1934 BY BREGMAN, VOCCO & CONN, INC. COPYRIGHT RENEWED 1961. ALL RIGHTS RESERVED. USED BY PERMISSION.

1. Sleigh-bells ring,   are you lis - t'nin'?   In the lane snow is
2. Gone a - way   is the blue - bird,   Here to stay is a
3. When it snows,   ain't it thrill - in'?   Tho' your nose gets a

glis - t'nin',   A beau - ti - ful sight,___   We're hap - py to - night,___
new bird,   He's sing - ing a song___   as we go a - long,___
chill - in',   We'll frol - ic and play___   the Es - ki - mo way,___

Fine

Walk - in' in a win - ter won - der - land!   land!

In the mead - ow we can build a snow - man,

And pre-tend that he's a cir - cus clown;   We'll have lots of fun with Mis - ter

D.C. al Fine

Snow - man, Un - til the oth - er kid - dies knock 'im down!

76 More About Form   *(To verse 3)*

A SIMPLE GIFT

WORDS AND MUSIC BY ROD McKUEN

Though the gift   be small   and   sim - ple,   if   the   wish   is
Let   it   be   a   sim - ple   gift then,   if   the   wish   is

wide,   Just   the   sim - ple   gift   of   giv - ing
wide,   Just   the   sim - ple   gift   of   giv - ing

makes you warm   in - side.____   Though   the thought   is
makes you warm   in - side.____

ev - er   fleet - ing,   if   a   thought   at   all,

Re - mem - ber ____   all the might - y   big things   start - ed   out   as small.____

So   if   you've   a   gift   worth   giv - ing,

let   it   be   your smile.____   Let   it   be   a

D.C. al Fine

kind - ly word ____   that makes the stran - ger   stop   a - while.

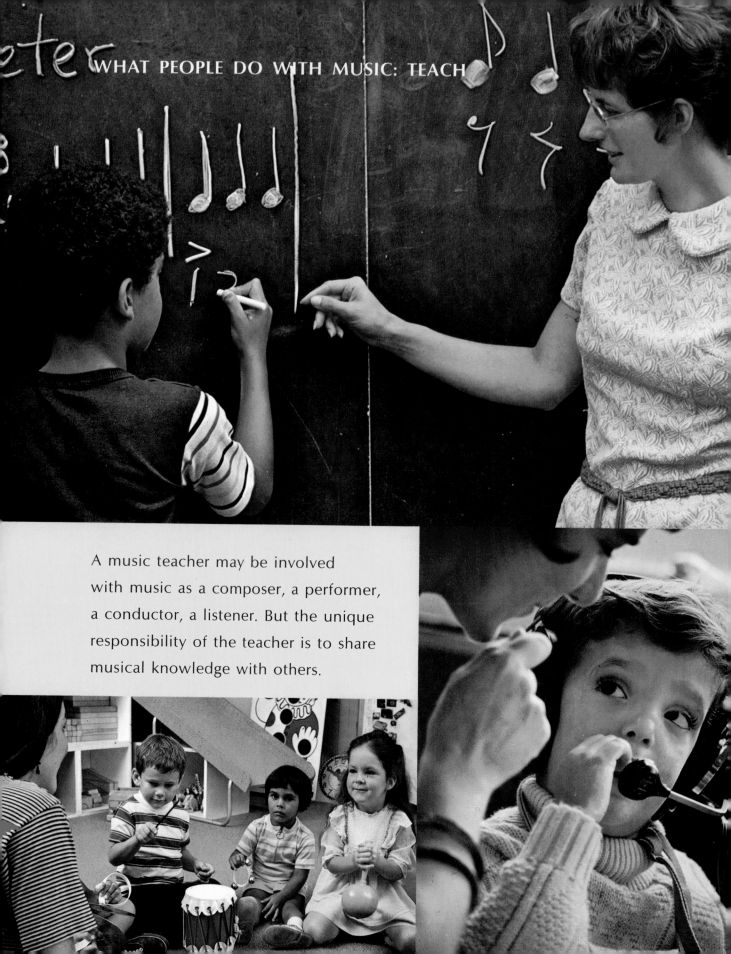

A music teacher may be involved
with music as a composer, a performer,
a conductor, a listener. But the unique
responsibility of the teacher is to share
musical knowledge with others.

For someone
who happens to like
both music and
people, being a
music teacher is
"having a good thing
going."

79

Interview one of the music teachers in your school or in the community. Here are some questions you might ask.

1 What made you decide to teach music?

2 How did you prepare to teach music?

3 What special area of music do you teach?

4 Besides teaching, what other musical roles are you involved with?

7 Can you think of a special incident that has happened in your teaching?

5 What do you find rewarding about teaching music?

6 What are the problems of being a music teacher?

SECTION 3
INTRODUCTION TO TONE COLOR

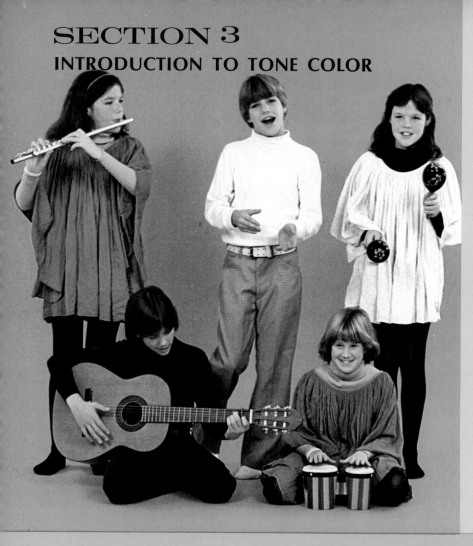

Sounds make music. Our world is filled with sounds, some natural, some from instruments invented to make sounds. This section will review some musical sounds—tone colors—that you know and add a few you might not know.

head
morning bed
city
song stone
lights
evening sings wings

Words, words, words. Just as music must have sounds, or tone colors, poetry must have words. The poet takes words and organizes them so they feel right together. What are some ways this poet organized his material—his words?

CITY 4

In the morning the city
Spreads its wings
Making a song
In stone that sings.

In the evening the city
Goes to bed
Hanging lights
About its head.

Langston Hughes

Music must have sounds—tone colors. Poetry must have words. Every art must have its basic materials.

USING WHAT YOU KNOW ABOUT TONE COLOR
Percussion Instruments

What tone colors do you hear at the very beginning of the recording of this song?

As you are learning the song, take turns making up an accompaniment on bongo drums.

WATER COME A ME EYE
FOLK SONG FROM JAMAICA

FROM FOLK SONGS OF JAMAICA (TOM MURRAY). COPYRIGHT 1952 BY THE OXFORD UNIVERSITY PRESS, LONDON. USED BY PERMISSION.

1. Ev - 'ry time I 'mem - ber Li - za,
2. Since you gone the days are lone - ly, Wa-ter come___ a me
3. When you here the time goes fast, ___

When I think 'bout my gal Li - za,
eye, Come back, gal, I love you on - ly, Wa-ter come___ a me
Now you gone and love is past, ___

eye. Come back, Li - za, come back, gal, ___

Wa - ter come___ a me eye. Come back, Li - za,

come back, gal, ___ Wa - ter come___ a me eye.

For a recorder ensemble, see p. 220.
For guitar fingerings, see p. 204.

Can you hear these percussion parts in the accompaniment on the recording of "Water Come a Me Eye"? Play one of the percussion parts while someone plays the other.

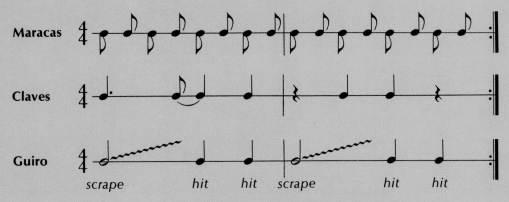

Add the tone color of the Autoharp or guitar playing harmony. If you play recorder, try adding the melody to the ensemble.

Practice your part alone before playing with others. When you are ready to perform, choose a leader to set a tempo and to start the group.

Listen to each part as you play so all the parts will *blend* (sound well together).

Here is another song to accompany with percussion instruments.

Play the tambourine accompaniment while learning the song.

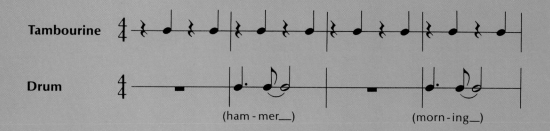

(ham - mer__)   (morn - ing__)

Continue playing the rhythm pattern at the end of each phrase.

THE HAMMER SONG

WORDS AND MUSIC BY LEE HAYS AND PETE SEEGER
TRO—© Copyright 1958 & 1962 LUDLOW MUSIC, INC., New York, N.Y. Used by permission

1. If I had a ham - mer,_____
2. If I had a bell,_____

I'd ham - mer in the morn - ing,_____
I'd ring it in the morn - ing,_____

I'd ham-mer in the eve - ning____ all o - ver this land;
I'd ring it in the eve - ning____ all o - ver this land;

I'd ham - mer out dan - ger,_____
I'd ring_____ out dan - ger,_____

I'd ham - mer out a warn - ing,_____
I'd ring_____ out a warn - ing,_____

I'd—— ham-mer out love be-tween my broth-ers and my sis-ters
I'd—— ring—— out love be-tween my broth-ers and my sis-ters

All _____ o - ver this land.____
All _____ o - ver this land.____

3. If I had a song, I'd sing it in the morning,
   I'd sing it in the evening all over this land;
   I'd sing out danger, I'd sing out a warning,
   I'd sing out love between my brothers and
       my sisters
   All over this land.

4. Well, I got a hammer and I got a bell,
   And I got a song to sing all over this land;
   It's the hammer of justice,
       it's the bell of freedom,
   It's the song about love between
       my brothers and my sisters
   All over this land.

📖 For a percussion ensemble, see p. 232.
📖 For guitar fingerings, see p. 204.

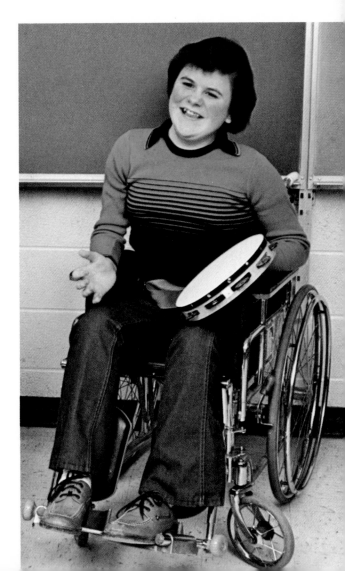

The Recorder

The photographs show the notes used in this piece for recorder. If you already know them, you are ready to play. If not, take time to practice the fingerings for B, A, and G.

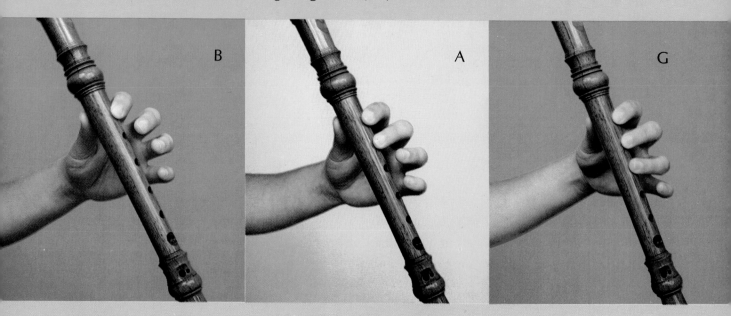

B   A   G

CARAVAN

MUSIC BY HELMUT BORNEFELD

"VIER LEICHTE STUCKE" FROM 25 EASY PIECES FOR SOPRANO RECORDER AND PIANO. USED BY PERMISSION OF BELWIN-MILLS PUBLISHING CORP. AS SOLE AGENTS FOR EDWIN F. KALMUS & CO., INC.

Ask a friend who plays the piano to practice the part included in your teacher's book. Add its tone color to the performance.

Listen to the tone color of recorders in this music. What percussion instruments are added?

Anonymous: *Five Villancicos,* "Pase el Agoa"

The Guitar

The guitar has never been more popular nor used more widely than it is today.

This page introduces you to an easy chord, E minor, which you can play to accompany some songs.

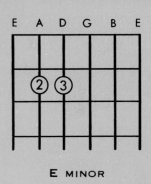

Look at the photograph to help you place the 2nd and 3rd fingers of your left hand on the strings. Which strings?

How far up on the strings will your fingers go?

Look at the diagram below to find the answers.

The 2nd and 3rd fingers are on the A and D strings between the 1st and 2nd frets.

To accompany this song, strum downward across the strings with the thumb of your right hand where you see the stroke (/).

E A D G B E

② ③

E MINOR

SHALOM CHAVERIM   FOLK ROUND FROM ISRAEL

Sha - lom, cha - ver - im! Sha - lom, cha - ver - im! Sha - lom, sha - lom! Le -

hit - ra - ot, le - hit - ra - ot, Sha - lom, sha - lom.

Other songs using the E minor chord are found in Playing the Guitar, p. 190.

The Voice

Your voice has its own tone color, whether you whisper, speak, shout, or sing. Perform one of your favorite songs as an example of your singing voice.

Now use your voice in a different way. Practice the first line of *Sound Piece 2,* which continues throughout the piece as an *ostinato.*

SOUND PIECE 2: Mouth Sounds   DORIS HAYS

© 1975 DORIS HAYS

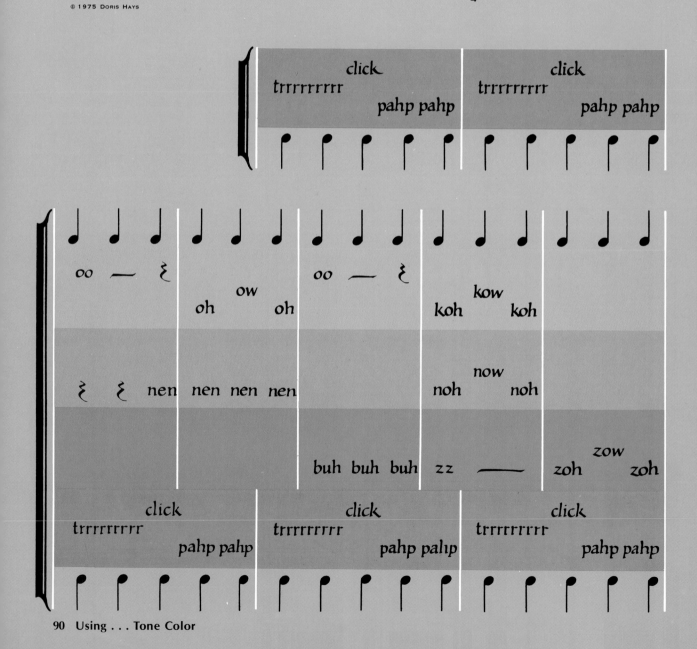

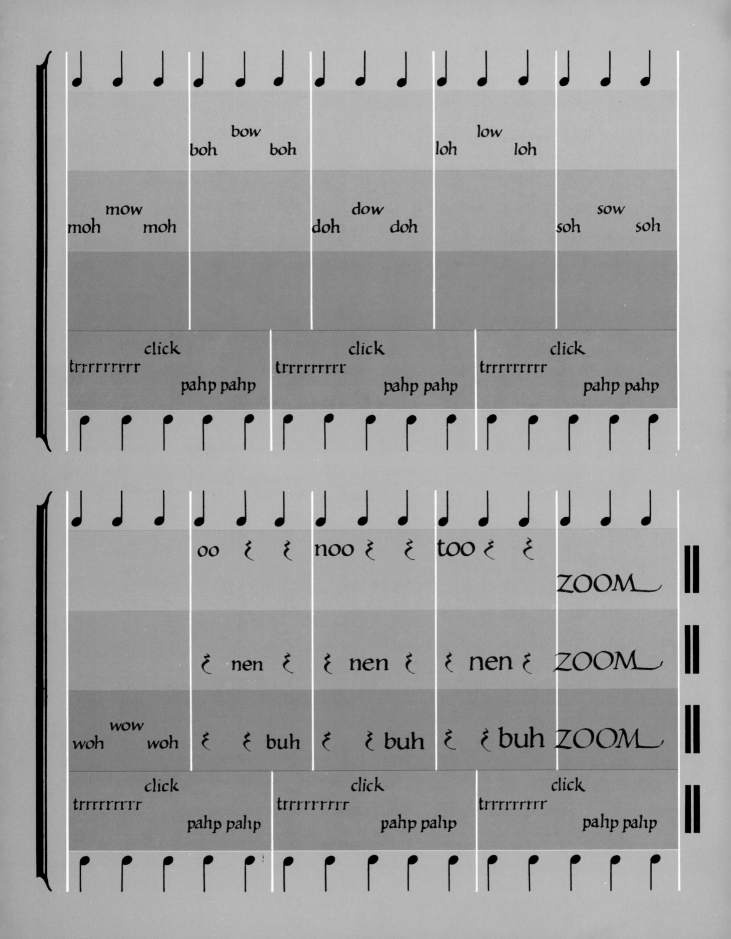

String Instruments

Listen to two of the instruments in the string family—violin and cello—in the recording of this song.

WINDS OF MORNING

WORDS AND MUSIC BY TOMMY MAKEM
COPYRIGHT © 1968 TOMMY MAKEM. USED BY PERMISSION OF TIN WHISTLE MUSIC, INC.

1. I've walked the hills___ when rain was fall - ing,___ Rest - ed
2. I've helped a plough - man tend his hors - es,___ Heard a

by a white oak tree, Heard a
rip - pling riv - er sing, Talked to

lark___ sing high at eve - ning,___ Caught a
stars___ when night was fall - ing,___ Seen a

moon - beam on the sea.___
prim - rose wel - come spring.___

REFRAIN

Soft - ly blow,___ ye winds of morn - ing;___ Sing, ye

winds,___ your mourn - ful sound. Blow ye

from___ the earth's four cor - ners;___ Guide this

trav - - 'ler where he's bound.

92   For guitar fingerings, see p. 204.

3. By foreign shores my feet have wandered,
    Heard a stranger call me friend;
    Every time my mind was troubled,
    Found a smile around the bend.
    Refrain

4. There's a ship stands in the harbor,
    All prepared to cross the foam;
    Far off hills were fair and friendly,
    Still there's fairer hills at home.
    Refrain

For a cello part, play open strings D, C, and G,
as indicated by the letters in the score.

For thicker density, add Autoharp or guitar,
using chords D, A, and G.

This piece is for a string orchestra.
Listen for the higher sounds of the violins
and violas, and the lower sounds of the cellos
and string basses. Tchaikowsky: *Serenade for Strings in C, "Waltz"*

Brass Instruments

What instrument of the brass family is playing the melody of this song?

CHRISTMAS IS COMING ENGLISH MELODY

1. Christ - mas is com - ing! The goose is get - ting fat!
2. If you've no pen - ny, A ha' - pen - ny will do,

Please to put a pen - ny in an old man's ___ hat,
If you have no ha' - pen - ny, Then God bless ___ you,

Please to put a pen - ny in an old man's hat.
If you have no ha' - pen - ny, Then God bless you.

Add these parts for trumpet and trombones to the tone color of the voices.

Trumpet

Trombone I

Trombone II

As you listen to this piece, you will hear the same melody
played at different times on different brass instruments. The chart
will tell you which instrument is playing the melody.

CALL CHART 5: Brass Instruments

Starer: *Five Miniatures for Brass, "Canon"*

1 TRUMPET	**4** FRENCH HORN
2 TRUMPET	**5** TROMBONE
3 TROMBONE	**6** TROMBONE IN LOW REGISTER

Woodwind Instruments

RAIN, RAIN, GO AWAY

WORDS AND MUSIC BY FRED STARK AND JERRY VANCE

1. I'm watching the clock on the wall counting the minutes away,
I can't wait to go spend the day with my friends.
Time goes so slow, don't you know when the rain's pouring down,
It's raining all over the ground, so I say:

2. Alone in my room by myself playing the record machine,
And looking for sunshine between all the clouds.
Where is the sun? It's no fun when the blue sky is gray.
I sure hope that Sunday will stay a sun day. *Refrain*

If you play flute or recorder, try either part in the refrain. If you play clarinet, practice this part to accompany the singing of the refrain.

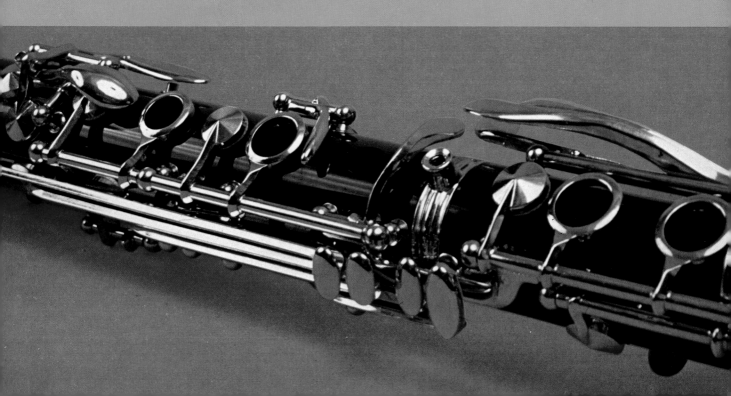

CALL CHART 6: Tone Color ⊙₄

In this Call Chart, you will hear the tone color of each of the woodwind instruments pictured. You will also hear a woodwind ensemble.

As each number is called, look at the pictures and listen to the sound.

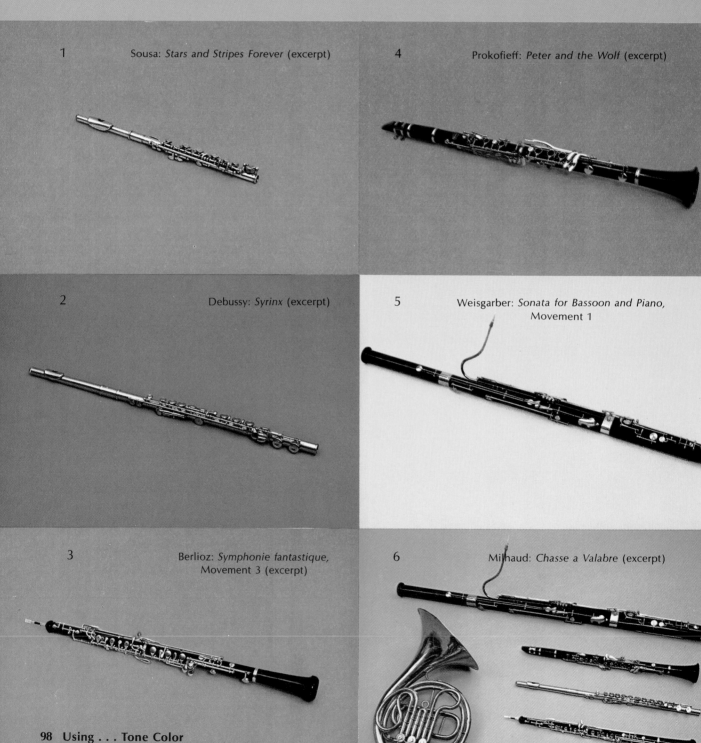

1   Sousa: *Stars and Stripes Forever* (excerpt)

4   Prokofieff: *Peter and the Wolf* (excerpt)

2   Debussy: *Syrinx* (excerpt)

5   Weisgarber: *Sonata for Bassoon and Piano,* Movement 1

3   Berlioz: *Symphonie fantastique,* Movement 3 (excerpt)

6   Milhaud: *Chasse a Valabre* (excerpt)

WHAT DO YOU HEAR? 4: Tone Color

These are tone colors you have heard or played. Do you hear one instrument, or a combination? On each line, circle what you hear.

1	VIOLIN	VIOLA	CELLO	STRING BASS	COMBINATION
2	GUITAR	AUTOHARP	RECORDER		COMBINATION
3	FLUTE	OBOE	CLARINET	BASSOON	COMBINATION
4	TRUMPET	TROMBONE	FRENCH HORN		COMBINATION
5	VIOLIN	VIOLA	CELLO	STRING BASS	COMBINATION
6	CHILDREN'S VOICES	MEN'S VOICES	WOMEN'S VOICES		COMBINATION
7	GUITAR	AUTOHARP	RECORDER		COMBINATION
8	MARACAS	CLAVES	DRUMS	GUIRO	COMBINATION
9	TRUMPET	TROMBONE	FRENCH HORN		COMBINATION
10	FLUTE	OBOE	CLARINET	BASSOON	COMBINATION

STYLE: NEW MUSIC

Using Instruments in New Ways

Composers have always been fascinated by new possibilities for sounds—
new ways to produce them and new ways to put them together.

Composers might use traditional instruments in unusual ways . . .
invent new instruments . . . create new sounds on an electronic
sound instrument . . . or change sounds with tape recorders.

In this piece you will hear traditional instruments—strings, brass, woodwinds, percussion—used in some new ways. Can you discover some of the ways?

5 Erb: *The Seventh Trumpet*

If you play an instrument used in that piece, experiment to find ways to make unusual sounds.

Voices can be used in unusual ways too. How many ways can you think of to make mouth sounds? Here are some. Try to think of others.

whispers	tongue clicks	lip-pops
shouts	moans	glides up and down

Can you create a piece using mouth and voice sounds? You might use a poem as part of it. You might build a score of the piece, such as:

poem with   lip-pops,   poem with
 moans,   tongue clicks SHOUTS   silence SHOUTS   moans,
 whispers   (loud)   whispers
 (soft)   (getting soft)

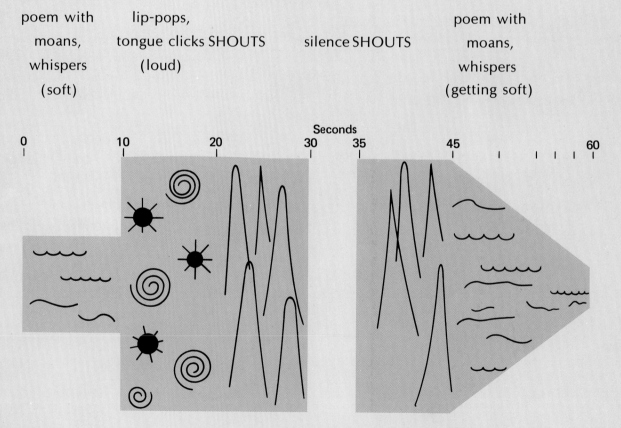

Another way to create new sounds with instruments or the voice is by amplification. A microphone can be placed in front of or directly on the sound maker. Connected to amplifiers that make the sound louder, the result is often an interesting new way to hear that instrument.

In this piece for jazz band you will hear sounds electrically amplified. How many of these instruments can you hear?

flute   clarinet   oboe
string bass   strings   piano
drums   saxophone   clarinet

🔘 **5** Withers: *Lean On Me*

You can make some interesting sounds if you have a microphone and speakers. Attach the microphone to various instruments and try making unusual sounds. Put the microphone on your throat. Try making different voice sounds and see what happens.

You can make an amplified sound piece, with a score such as the one on p. 102. Try tape-recording your piece to play for others, asking them to guess how the sounds were made.

Inventing New Instruments

As composers look for new ways to make sounds, they sometimes invent new instruments.

Composer Harry Partch was not satisfied with just 12 tones within the octave, nor with the instruments that are built to play the 12 tones.

He invented his own instruments on which he could play 43 different tones within one octave. A picture of one of Mr. Partch's inventions—the cloud chamber bowls—is shown below.

Listen to a piece he composed for the cloud chamber bowls—large, 12-gallon glass bottles sawed in half. Each half is hung from a wire and struck with small, soft mallets.

 Partch: *Cloud Chamber Music*
5

When you listen again, hear what makes the contrast in the second section.

1. strong, steady beat   *3.* contrast of tone color

2. melody played in several registers   4. use of singing voice

Another composer of new music is featured in *What People Do with Music-Compose*, p. 124.

Try inventing instruments out of a variety of materials: tin cans, glasses, bottles, pot lids, etc.

Work in small groups to put together sounds. Try to get a musical result. Think of ways to notate your piece for others to play.

Using the Voice in New Ways

Use the tone color of your voice to recite this poem.

NIGHT SOUNDS

Night sounds
Depending where
Are very different
Loud and soft but never complete
Silence

David S. Walker

Now say the poem in a different way, adding one of the tone colors shown below.

SOUND PIECE 3: Night Sounds

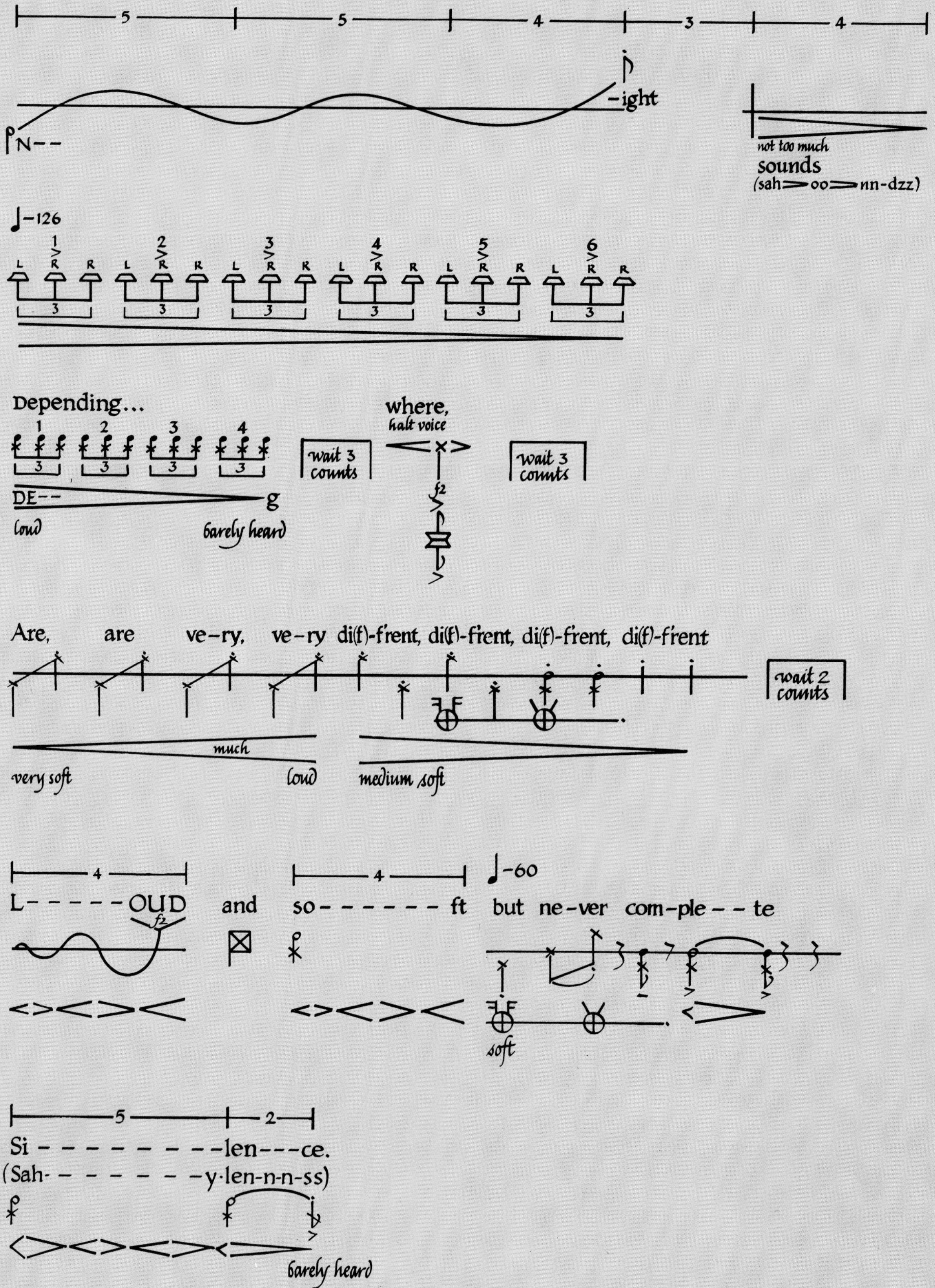

Depending...

where,
half voice

wait 3 counts

DE-- loud   barely heard

Are,   are   ve-ry,   ve-ry di(f)-frent, di(f)-frent, di(f)-frent, di(f)-frent

wait 2 counts

very soft   much   loud   medium soft

L - - - - - OUD   and   so - - - - - - ft   but ne-ver com-ple - - te

soft

Si - - - - - - - - len---ce.
(Sah- - - - - - -y·len-n-n-ss)

barely heard

To perform this sound piece, follow the explanation of the symbols in the legend. Use the recording to help you.

Listen to how one composer uses voices in unusual ways to imitate frogs, toads, insects, screech owls, and the murmur of a breeze.

○ Ravel: *L'Enfant et les Sortilèges,* "Andante," excerpt

EXPERIENCING THE ARTS: ORNAMENTATION

An *ornament* is a decoration added to "dress up" something. Can you find some things in the room that are "dressed up," or embellished, or decorated?

Can you find some things that do not use decorations—things that are not "dressed up"? Some things have ornamentation and some do not.

Look at these pictures and those on pages 112 and 113. Can you describe the ornaments used—or their lack of use—in each pair?

CHINESE SCULPTURE. SINGLE FIGURE OF MAITREYA. THE METROPOLITAN MUSEUM OF ART. KENNEDY FUND. 1926.

CHINESE SCULPTURE. MAITREYA ALTARPIECE. THE METROPOLITAN MUSEUM OF ART. ROGERS FUND. 1938.

Ornamentation in Music

A melody can be ornamented too, by adding extra tones to "dress it up." If you know the melody and listen for it, you can better appreciate the ornaments added to it.

Here is a melody for you to sing. Learn it so you can sing it from memory.

AMAZING GRACE   EARLY AMERICAN MELODY   WORDS BY JOHN NEWTON

1. A - maz - ing___ grace, how sweet the sound
2. The Lord has___ prom - ised good to me,

That saved a___ wretch like me!_____
His word my___ hope se - cures;_____

I once_____ was___ lost, but now_____ am___ found,
He will_____ my___ shield and por - tion___ be

Was blind, but___ now I see._____
As long as___ life en - dures._____

The melody of "Amazing Grace" can be ornamented by adding extra tones to it. One way to add extra tones is to fill in some or all the tones between two melody notes

The_____ Lord

or leave the melody note and return to it.

pro - mised

Here is an example of how a gospel singer ornaments the melody of "Amazing Grace." Listen to it and follow the words and the music. Half notes (♩) are used on the same syllables as in the original melody to help you keep your place.

Amazing Grace, ornamented version

2. The ____ Lord, the ____ Lord, ____

The _____ Lord has___ prom - ised, promised good_____ to__

me,__ His___ word my____ hope_____ se - cures;_____ He_____

will _____ my shield_____ and__

por - tion, por-tion be_____ As___ long,____

as long,_____ as__ long__ as__ life_____

life_____ en - dures._____

MORE ABOUT TONE COLOR
Gamelan Orchestra of Indonesia

Gamelans are orchestras in Indonesia composed of percussion, string, and wind instruments.

🔘 **5** Hudan Mas (Golden Rain)

Kempul

Ketuk

Gong Ageng

Kenong

Learn to play a short piece of gamelan music. Play the following phrases on bells, glockenspiels, or metallophones. Notice that each phrase repeats. As you play, keep the rhythm steady.

F   A   B♭   A   B♭   A   C   B♭

F   E   F   E   F   E   C   B♭

Other players add the tone color of a variety of gongs played on certain beats of the melody phrase. The gongs are pictured on p. 116.

Beats	1	2	3	4	5	6	7	8
Gong Ageng								x
Kenong		x		x		x		x
Kempul			x		x		x	
Ketuk	x	x	x	x	x	x	x	

These gongs can be made from kitchen pots and pans and the lids. Experiment with different ways to strike them.

Put all the parts together—melody played on glockenspiels or bells, accompanied by the gongs.

Ipu and Pu-ili Sticks of Hawaii

In Hawaii, some instruments are made from gourds and bamboo.
The *ipu* is a large hollow gourd that is struck with the heel of
the hand and the tips of the fingers. Play this pattern on the ipu.

♩ = play with tips of fingers

♪ = play with heel of hand

NANI WALE NA HALA

FOLK SONG FROM HAWAII

ENGLISH VERSION BY ALICE FIRGAU

Na - ni wa - le na ha - la,   E - a, e - a.
Ke___ on - i a   e - la,

O Na - u - e i - ke ka - i,   E - a, e - a.
Pi - li ma - i Ha - e - na,

Lovely are the hala trees, **Ea, ea.**
Swaying by the gentle seas, **Ea, ea.**

Near Haena halas grow, **Ea, ea.**
In Naue breezes blow, **Ea, ea.**

The tapping of *pu-ili* sticks adds a special tone color to that of
the ipu. A pu-ili stick is a piece of bamboo that is fringed on
one end to make the stick flexible.

Figure out the pattern for each phrase.

Verse 1:

		PATTERN A		
Tap sticks together in front.	Tap sticks on floor to side.	Tap sticks in front.	Tap sticks on floor.	Repeat.
Tap sticks together overhead.	Tap right shoulder with right stick.	Tap sticks overhead.	Tap left shoulder with left stick.	Repeat.

Verse 2:
Tap crossed sticks overhead from right to left.

				Repeat from left to right.
Tap sticks overhead.	Tap right shoulder with right stick.	Tap sticks overhead.	Tap left shoulder with left stick.	Repeat.

For guitar fingerings, see p. 204.

Koto of Japan

In Japan, the tone color of the koto is well known. Listen to the koto playing the accompaniment of this melody.

SAKURA   FOLK SONG FROM JAPAN   MODERN ARRANGEMENT BY HENRY BURNETT   ENGLISH VERSION BY LORENE HOYT

1. Sa - ku - ra,   Sa - ku - ra,   Cher - ry blos - soms
2. Sa - ku - ra,   Sa - ku - ra,   Blos - soms wav - ing
   Sa - ku - ra,   Sa - ku - ra,   Ya - yo - i   no

ev - 'ry - where.   Clouds of glo - ry fill the___ sky,
in the___ breeze.   Yo - shi - no,   the cher - ry___ land,
so - ra___ wa,   Mi - wa - ta - su   ka - gi - ri,

Mist of beau - ty in the___ air,   Love - ly col - ors float - ing___ by,
Tat - su - ta, the ma - ple___ trees,   Ka - ra - sa - ki, pine tree___ grand,
Ka - su - mi ka ku - mo - ka,   Ni - o - i zo i - zu - ru;

Sa - ku - ra,   Sa - ku - ra,   Let___ all come___ sing - ing.
Sa - ku - ra,   Sa - ku - ra,   Let___ all come___ sing - ing.
I - za - ya,   i - za - ya Mi___ ni   yu - kan._____

Now listen to the tone color of the koto playing alone. How does the composer use the "Sakura" melody to form a piece?

Eto: Variations on Sakura

For a dance, see p. 250.

STYLE: ESKIMO AND AMERICAN INDIAN SONG

When Christopher Columbus arrived in America, he was already a latecomer—the Indians and the Eskimos had been living here for thousands of years.

Television and movies usually give us just one view of the American Indian—that of the Plains Indian with his feathered bonnets, horses, tepees, buffalo hunting, and warfare.

However, the way of life of the Indian and the Eskimo showed much variety. Some were wandering hunters; others settled in villages and grew crops. Some were warlike; others were peaceful. Some groups had kings; others had headmen. Some were guided in their religious lives by priests; others had guardian spirits.

The music of the Indians and the Eskimos also showed much variety. Three different kinds of Indian music are from places pictured on the map.

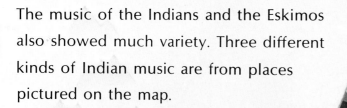

Within each of these areas, the music is somewhat alike, but from one area to another it can be very different.

The Eskimo

The way of life and languages of the Eskimo are quite different
from Indians. The Eskimos live all across the top of the
North American continent. They survive in the very harsh climate
of the far north by hunting and by fishing. They adapt to their climate
through clever inventions like the igloo and the kayak.

The Eskimo's most important musical instrument is a large, shallow
tambourine drum covered with caribou skin.

Other instruments such as rattles, flutes, and whistles
are sometimes found, but by far the most important form of music
is the song accompanied by the drum.

As you listen to this Eskimo song about a musk ox hunt,
answer these questions.

1. Is the range of pitches narrow, or wide?
2. Is the tempo slow, or fast?
3. How would you describe the tone color of the voices?

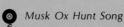 *Musk Ox Hunt Song*

Other Eskimo songs often
comment on the problems
of life, including how hard
it is to make up songs!

The Navajo

The Navajo Indians live on a reservation that lies in parts of Arizona, New Mexico, and Utah. They raise sheep and grow crops and are widely known for their weaving and their silverwork.

This song is part of the Night Chant, or Yeibichei, an important nine-day ceremony in which boys and girls are initiated into the religious life of the tribe.

Listen to discover how the voices in this song are different from the Eskimo song. ⊙ *Night Chant Song*

When you listen again, answer some other questions.

1. What instrument accompanies the voices?
2. Is the beat steady?
3. What is the tempo?
4. Is the range of pitches wide, or narrow?
5. Does the melody focus on one important tone?

All of these qualities make up a style that is very different from that of the Eskimos.

The Salish

In Western Montana, between the Navajos and the Eskimos, live the Salish Indians. Their music and dance, often centered traditionally on ideas of war, are clearly in the style of Plains Indians.

The kind of music the Salish sang—and still sing—in their *War Dance Song* is the same type sung by other Plains Indians such as the Sioux, Cheyenne, Arapaho, and Blackfeet. It is also the kind of music we usually hear on television or in the movies when Indians are shown.

Listen to a *War Dance Song* sung by a mixed group of Salish and Blackfeet Indians. What are some of the things you hear?

◉
6 *War Dance Song*

Not all Eskimo music sounds like the *Musk Ox Hunt Song,* or all Navajo music like the *Night Chant,* or all Salish music like the *War Dance Song.*

Much variety exists in the music of each of these societies.

The music of all these groups is changing. What you have heard is traditional song, but the Indians and Eskimos of today sing and play other types of music— guitar songs, rock, jazz, country-Western, classical, and all the other kinds of music found in the United States.

Music always changes, and music in Indian and Eskimo societies is changing too.

Many composers today use traditional instruments in unusual ways, or they find or invent sound sources. On the recording, Donald Erb tells how he composes. You will hear *Trio for Two* and a piece he composed for you, *Nightmusic for Nine*.

What People Do with Music: Compose
6

SOUND PIECE 4:

NIGHTMUSIC FOR NINE <small>DONALD ERB</small>

Scored for:

1. Autoharp or piano (One player); Mark end of strings with colored tape for easy identification.

2. Harmonica in C. Cover all the E's with small strips of masking tape.

3. Five 10 oz. pop bottles partially filled with water, to be tuned as shown and placed in order from left to right. (Five players)

4. Maracas (One player); Slide whistle (One player).

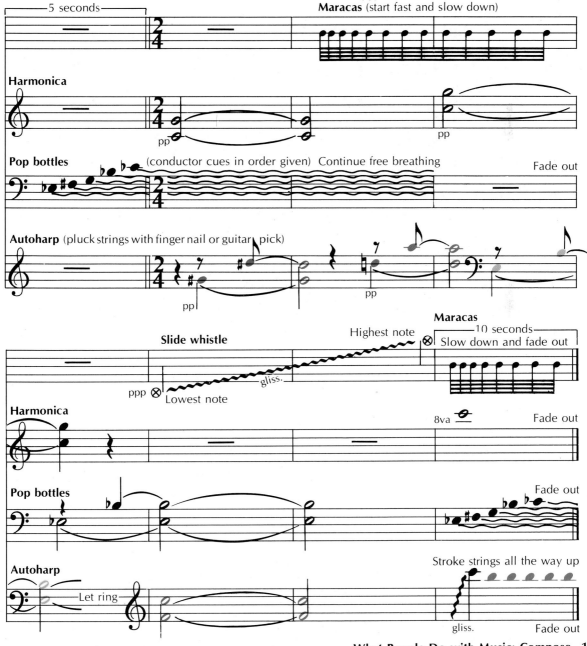

SECTION: 4

INTRODUCTION TO MELODY, HARMONY, TEXTURE

Glance very quickly at this painting.
Look up as soon as you recognize
what it is. What did you see?

Now look at the painting again,
but this time very carefully and
slowly. Notice as many details
about it as you can. Think about
how the painting uses these qualities:

colors	lines
shapes	directions
repetitions	depth
contrasts	distortion

Now listen to a piece of music.
As it is playing, read pages 128
and 129 in your books. Try to get as
much from your reading as you can.

Haydn: *Symphony 45,* Movement 3 (excerpt)

Now listen again. *Listen hard.*
Try to hear how the music
uses these qualities:

tempo	repetitions
beat	contrasts
meter	tone colors
longer and	steps and leaps
shorter notes	

The more things you really see in a painting, the more you will enjoy it.

The more things you hear in music, the more you will enjoy it.

This section will help you bring three qualities of music into focus—*melody, harmony,* and *texture.*

Melody is the way single tones are played, one after the other. We can picture melody with a line that shows its contour.

Harmony is the way tones are sounded together, usually chords that accompany a melody.

Two or more melodies can be played at the same time.

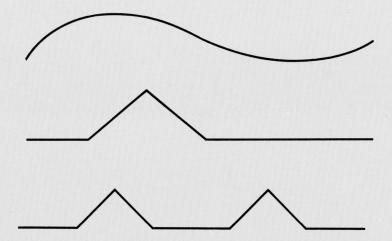

Texture is the way melodies and harmonies work together.

You'll explore some of these ways to enjoy music in this section.

Works of art want to make us look "hard," listen "hard," think and feel "hard." It takes some work to enjoy art. Thinking more lets us feel more.

USING WHAT YOU KNOW ABOUT MELODY, HARMONY, TEXTURE

Melody Contour

As you listen to this song, follow the contour of the melody.

Which line shows the contour of the first phrase?

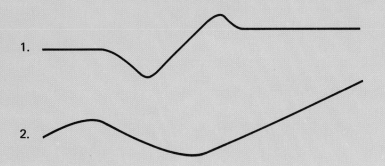

1.

2.

THE MUSIC IS YOU

WORDS AND MUSIC BY JOHN DENVER

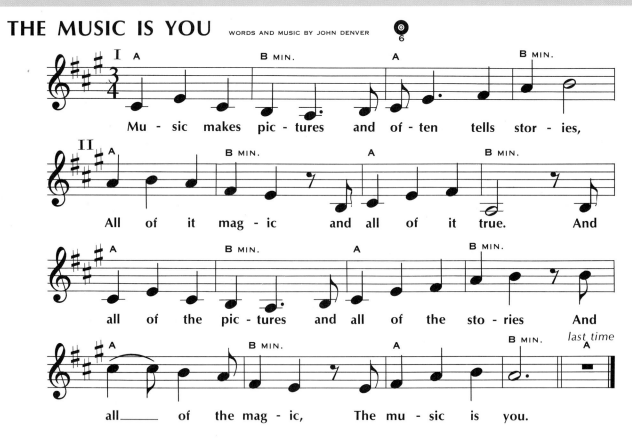

Mu - sic makes pic - tures and of - ten tells stor - ies,

All of it mag - ic and all of it true. And

all of the pic - tures and all of the sto - ries And

all___ of the mag - ic, The mu - sic is you.

Sing the song as a two-part round to hear the texture of two
lines of melody working together.

Intervals

The special contour of each melody is created by *intervals*—the distance between tones. As you sing the echo parts throughout the B section of the song, notice how some tones repeat, some move upward or downward by steps, and some leap upward or downward.

THE OCEAN WAVES

FOLK SONG FROM GREECE   ENGLISH WORDS BY MARIA JORDAN

1. The o-cean waves, the o-cean waves are az-ure blue._____ Their rock-ing
2. The o-cean waves, the o-cean waves, they splash their dew._____ And drops fall

mo-tion lul-la-bies my love to sleep._____ She slum-bers in my
ev-'ry-where no mat-ter what you do._____ Rock gent-ly 'gainst my

fish-ing boat. Be still, or she may wak-en._____
lit-tle boat. A spe-cial some-one's sleep-ing!_____

(Waves come and go)   (all day and night)
Waves come and go_____ all day and night._____ Waves come and

(echo each time)
go_____ through dark and light._____ The tide comes in,_____ the tide moves

out._____ A won-drous thing_____ with-out a doubt._____

For another song from Greece, see p. 244.
For a percussion part, see p. 233.

Using . . . Melody, Harmony, Texture **129**

Comparing Two Melodies

Sometimes a folk singer has to choose between different versions of the same song. Here is an English ballad sung two ways. Listen to the two versions and choose one to sing.

Although the story remains the same, the music sounds different.

SCARBOROUGH FAIR   FOLK SONG FROM ENGLAND

VERSION ONE

1. Are you go - ing to Scar - bor - ough fair,
2. Tell her to make me a cam - bric shirt,
3. Tell her to wash it in yon - der well,

Pars - ley, sage, rose-ma - ry, and thyme; With - out any seam— or
Re - mem - ber me— to
Where never spring wa - ter nor

one who lives there,
nee - dle work, For once she was a true love of mine.
rain ev - er fell,

SCARBOROUGH FAIR

FOLK SONG FROM ENGLAND

VERSION TWO

In which version are the melody phrases all different?

In which version is there repetition of melody phrases? Which version is major? Which is minor?

What is the meter of each version?

Which version is performed faster?

These are some things to look for when analyzing a melody. Try analyzing other melodies in this book, including the Chorus and Recorder Satellites.

Look for phrases, repetitions, contrasts, major and minor, meter, tempo.

The more you analyze the better you will understand how the melody makes musical sense.

Register

SOUND PIECE 5 :Walkin' Talkin' Blues   DORIS HAYS

This score shows patterns of high and low sounds in a different way. To read it, follow the circles in the direction of the arrows.

Can you compose a sound piece of your own?

High and Low Registers

Some parts for keyboard are played in a high register and some in a low register.

If you play the piano, practice the high part, called *Primo,* in this duet. Ask someone to play the low part, called *Secondo,* with you.

Russian Folk Song   Peter Ilyitch Tchaikowsky

High, Middle, and Low Register

Choose one of the phrases in this round to play on the piano.

Use high, middle, or low register as shown by the keyboard diagram.

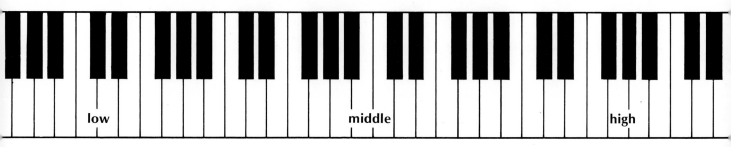

EVERYBODY LOVES SATURDAY NIGHT   FOLK SONG FROM GHANA

Ev - 'ry - bod - y loves Sat - ur - day night,

Ev - 'ry - bod - y loves Sat - ur - day night.

Ev - 'ry-bod-y, Ev - 'ry-bod-y, Ev - 'ry-bod-y, Ev - 'ry-bod-y,

Ev - 'ry - bod - y loves Sat - ur - day night.

Ask three friends to play the other phrases with you. Play them one after the other to hear the melody. Then play any two phrases together, then three, then four.

Another time, try playing the steady beat in the lowest register.

Play low C four times, followed by low G. Alternate throughout the song.

For guitar fingerings, see p. 204.

Fugue

In this piece for organ you will hear a melody, called a *subject,* played in different registers. It is woven together with countermelodies as the music moves along. This piece is written in a special form called *fugue.*

Follow the chart to help your mind perceive what you hear.

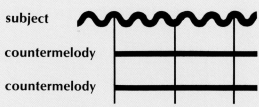

CALL CHART 7: Register Pachelbel: *Fugue No. 3 on Magnificat*

1 〰〰〰 SUBJECT ALONE IN MIDDLE REGISTER

2 SUBJECT IN HIGHER REGISTER, ONE COUNTERMELODY

3 SUBJECT IN HIGHEST REGISTER, TWO COUNTERMELODIES

4 SUBJECT IN LOW REGISTER, COUNTERMELODIES ABOVE

5 SUBJECT IN MIDDLE REGISTER, ONE COUNTERMELODY ABOVE, ONE BELOW

6 SUBJECT IN HIGHER REGISTER, TWO COUNTERMELODIES

7 SUBJECT IN HIGHEST REGISTER, TWO COUNTERMELODIES

8 SUBJECT IN LOW REGISTER, COUNTERMELODIES ABOVE

9 SUBJECT IN LOWEST REGISTER, COUNTERMELODIES ABOVE

Melody with Accompaniment

A melody can be sung or played alone, or it can have an accompaniment. After singing these melodies, add an accompaniment on the guitar. They use the E minor chord, which you learned on p. 89.

HEY, HO! NOBODY HOME OLD ENGLISH ROUND

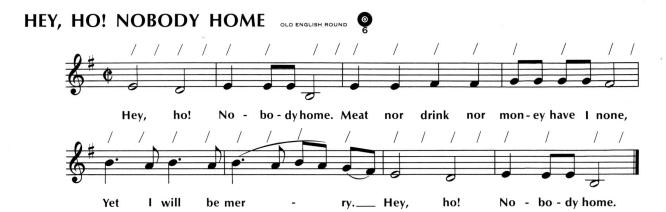

Hey, ho! No - bo - dy home. Meat nor drink nor mon - ey have I none,

Yet I will be mer - ry. ___ Hey, ho! No - bo - dy home.

This song uses two melodies, one in Section A and one in Section B. When sung together, they make a melody with countermelody.

ZUM GALI GALI FOLK SONG FROM ISRAEL

Zum ga - li ga - li, ga - li, Zum ga - li ga - li,

Zum ga - li ga - li, ga - li, Zum ga - li ga - li.

1. He - cha - lutz l' - man a - vo - dah; ___
2. A - vo - dah l' - man he - cha - lutz; ___

___ A - vo - dah l' - man he - cha - lutz.
___ He - cha - lutz l' - man a - vo - dah.

For directions for dancing the hora, see p. 243.

Melody; Accompaniment; Countermelody

Listen to the recording to hear how this melody is performed. Is it melody alone? Melody with accompaniment? Melody with countermelody?

VINE AND FIG TREE

MUSIC BY SHALOM ALTMAN   HEBREW WORDS FROM ISAIAH 2:4

ENGLISH VERSION BY LEAH JAFFA AND FRAN MINKOFF

WORDS AND MELODY COPYRIGHT © 1948 BY SHALOM ALTMAN   USED BY PERMISSION

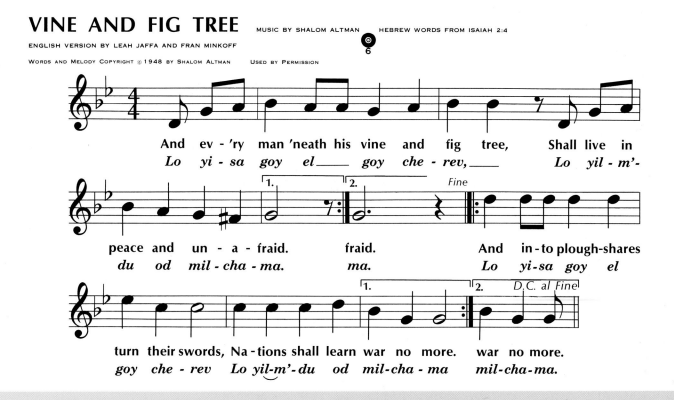

And ev - 'ry man 'neath his vine and fig tree, Shall live in
Lo yi - sa goy el___ goy che - rev,___ Lo yil - m'-

peace and un - a - fraid.   fraid.   And in - to plough-shares
du od mil - cha - ma.   ma.   Lo yi - sa goy el

turn their swords, Na - tions shall learn war no more.   war no more.
goy che - rev Lo yil-m'- du od mil-cha - ma   mil-cha-ma.

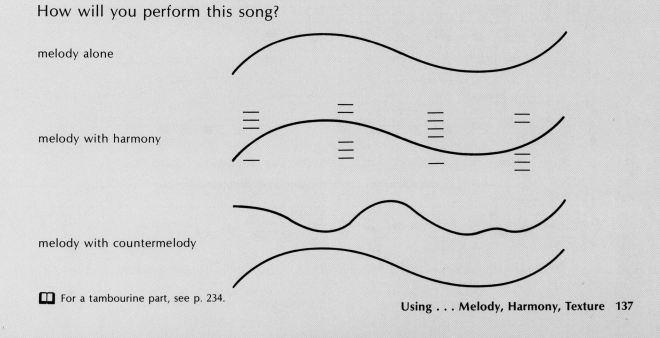

The way melody and harmony are organized to sound together creates texture in music.

How will you perform this song?

melody alone

melody with harmony

melody with countermelody

For a tambourine part, see p. 234.

Using . . . Melody, Harmony, Texture 137

Melody with Accompaniment

Listen to the recording. Do you hear melody alone, or melody with accompaniment?

YOU'RE MY FRIEND

WORDS AND MUSIC BY CHRIS DEDRICK

© 1972 ALMITRA MUSIC COMPANY. INC.

INTRODUCTION

You're my friend.___ You're my friend.___

You're my friend. _____

VERSE

1. Just this morn-in' we went fish-in';

Could-n't e-ven find a worm for bait._____

Nev-er had more fun,___ Nev-er laughed so hard,___

Nev-er knew a one___ like you for mak-in' "no bait" fish-in' feel so great.___

'Cause you're my friend.___ You're my friend.___

You're my friend___ till the end, You're my friend.___

CODA (last time only)   rit.

You're my friend. ___   You're my friend. ___

2. Remember when I threw a snowball;
   Broke the Christmas light upon your tree?
   How your dad did yell, How I ran away,
   Why did you go tell him that you did it?
   You were punished 'stead of me.
   'Cause you're my friend. You're my friend.
   You're my friend till the end, You're my friend.

3. Hate to see you move away now.
   Listen to the sad call of the wren.
   Some ol' lucky guy will be your new-found friend,
   Love you just as I have—In my mind
   You'll be beside me till the end.
   'Cause you're my friend. You're my friend.
   You're my friend till the end, You're my friend.
   (*To Coda*)

When you know the song, add chords played on the keyboard
or bells. Play alone or with a friend.

Start with chord 1, which is played in every measure indicated
by * in the score. Otherwise, play chord 2.

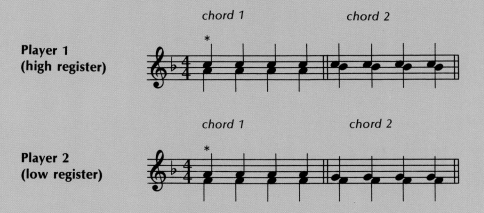

Player 1
(high register)

Player 2
(low register)

SOUND PIECE 6: JUNCTURE DANCE 1

Doris Hays

© 1975 Doris Hays

Look at the score of this sound piece to find the separate parts that move horizontally (side to side). When these parts are played together, they "fit" and support each other.

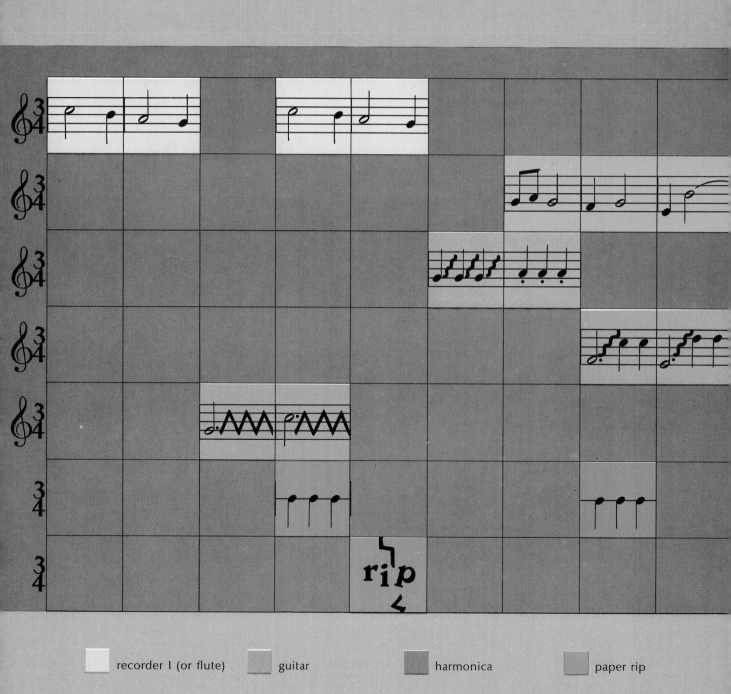

recorder I (or flute)　　guitar　　harmonica　　paper rip

For recorder fingerings, see p. 251.

Autoharp: 〜〜 means to strum. Let the strings sound for the full value of the note. Pluck the two quarter notes.

Harmonica: ⋀⋀⋀ means to blow with a puffy sound, both in and out.

Paper rip: rip slowly so the sound lasts for three beats.

Memorize your part. Try other arrangements of the color blocks.

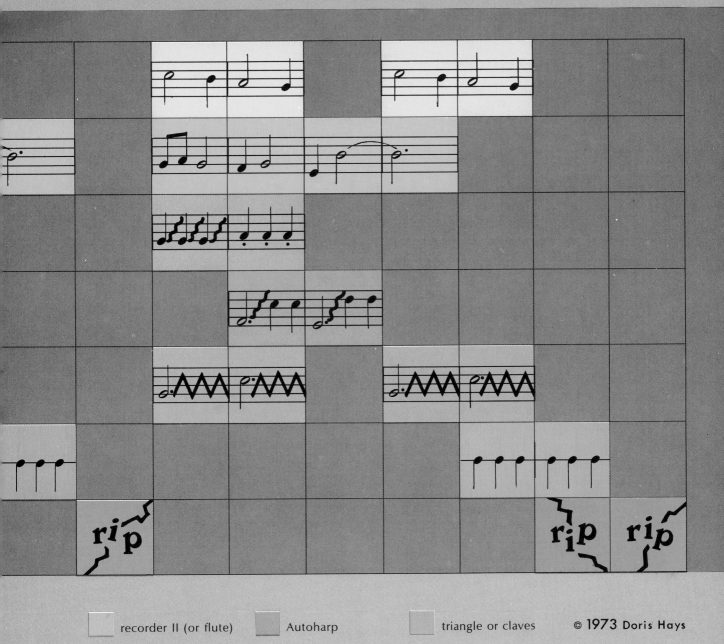

recorder II (or flute)   Autoharp   triangle or claves   © 1973 Doris Hays

Music with Different Textures

Listen to the recording to hear how different textures are used.

- chord introduction
- melody overlapping (canon—like a round)
- melody alone
- melody overlapping
- melody with harmony and countermelody played by an oboe

MEE Y'MALEYL

HEBREW FOLK MELODY   ENGLISH VERSION BY JUDITH K. EISENSTEIN

FROM THE GATEWAY TO JEWISH SONG   © 1939 BY BEHRMAN'S JEWISH BOOK HOUSE, NEW YORK   USED BY PERMISSION

Mee y'-ma-leyl g'vu-rot Yis-ra-eyl? O - tan mee yim - neh?
Who can re-tell the things that be-fell us? Who can count them?

Heyn, b'-chal dor ya-kum ha-gib-bor Go - eyl ha - am.
In ev-'ry age a he - ro or sage came to our aid.

Sh'ma!   Ba - ya-meem ha-heym ba-z'man ha - zeh,
Ah!   At this time of year in days of yore,

Ma - ka-bee mo-shee - a u-fo-deh.   Uv'-ya-mey-nu kal am Yis-ra-
Mac-ca-bees the tem-ple did re-store.   And to-day our peo-ple, as we

D.C. al Fine

eyl,   Yit - a - hkheyd ya-kum l'-hig-ga-eyl.
dreamed,   Will a - rise, u - nite, and be re-deemed.

Tambourine   etc.

Drum   etc.

Play this bell part throughout "Christmas Canon" to create a different texture.

CHRISTMAS CANON   WORDS AND MUSIC BY DAVID EDDLEMAN

I F   C₇   F   C₇

See him slum - b'ring in_____ the hay, He's

II F   C₇   F   C₇

sleep - ing at the close of day. Come

III F   C₇   F   C₇

sing his praise_____ to God_____ on_____ high, But

IV F   C₇   F

sing soft - ly, sing.

ALLELUIA, AMEN   TRADITIONAL ROUND

I

Al - le - lu - ia, al - le - lu - ia.

II

A - _____ men, a - men.

Accompany the singing of "Alleluia, Amen" by playing this countermelody, called a *peal,* on the bells.

STYLE: A MUSICAL IDEA IN VARIOUS STYLES

A melody can be varied, too. Some of the ways are to change rhythm, tempo, dynamics, tone color, and texture.

Often there is no one right way—one "proper style"—for a melody. Each way adds a musical flavor of its own.

Follow the score as you listen to a melody played alone.

GREENSLEEVES FOLK SONG FROM ENGLAND

Here is a sound collage using the same melody in different styles.
The chart will help you hear how texture and tone color are used.

What other differences can you hear in the various styles—in
rhythm, in tempo, in dynamics?

CALL CHART 8: STYLE 🎧 *Greensleeves*

TEXTURE	TONE COLOR
1 Melody with Accompaniment	Guitar
2 Melody with Accompaniment	Voices, English Horn, Guitar, Finger Cymbals
3 Melody with Accompaniment	Strings, Harp, Flute
4 Melody Alone	Carillon (Bells)
5 Melody with Accompaniment	Voice, Lute
6 Melody with Countermelody	Woodwinds

In addition to all the other ways *Greensleeves* has been used, it
has also been sung with different words. Which version will you sing?

Alas, my love, you do me wrong
To cast me off discourteously,
And I have loved you too long,
Delighting in your company.

Greensleeves is all my joy,
Greensleeves is my delight,
Greensleeves is my heart of gold
And who but my Lady Greensleeves?"

Style: A Musical Idea in Various Styles 145

WHAT PEOPLE DO WITH MUSIC: PERFORM

7

For more about the guitar, see "Playing the Guitar," beginning on p. 189.

Today's performer is likely to be equally familiar with recording studios and concert halls.

David Spinozza plays all styles from classical guitar to rock. On the recording, he tells some of the many ways he performs music.

MORE ABOUT MELODY, HARMONY, TEXTURE
Sequences

Follow the score as you listen to this song to hear phrases
repeated at different pitch levels, called *sequences*.

ISLAND HOPPING   FOLK SONG FROM GREECE   ENGLISH WORDS BY MARIA JORDAN

1. Bags are packed and all is rea - dy, can't wait___ to
   Boat is board-ing at the jet - ty, soon we'll___ de -

start; (can't wait___ to start;)
part; (soon we'll___ de - part;)

Is - land hop - ping we___ are___ go - ing,

Sea is calm, a soft___ wind's___ blow - ing,

We can feel ex - cite - ment___ grow - ing

in ev - 'ry heart,___ *Ahs-tohkah-loh*___ In ev - 'ry___ heart.

When you know the song, try singing the harmony part. It
follows the contour of the melody, but starts on a higher pitch.

How many things can you hear in the melody phrases of this Basque folk song? The symbol or word in the chart will tell you what happens in each phrase.

Begiak, Barres, Barres

CALL CHART 9: Sequences

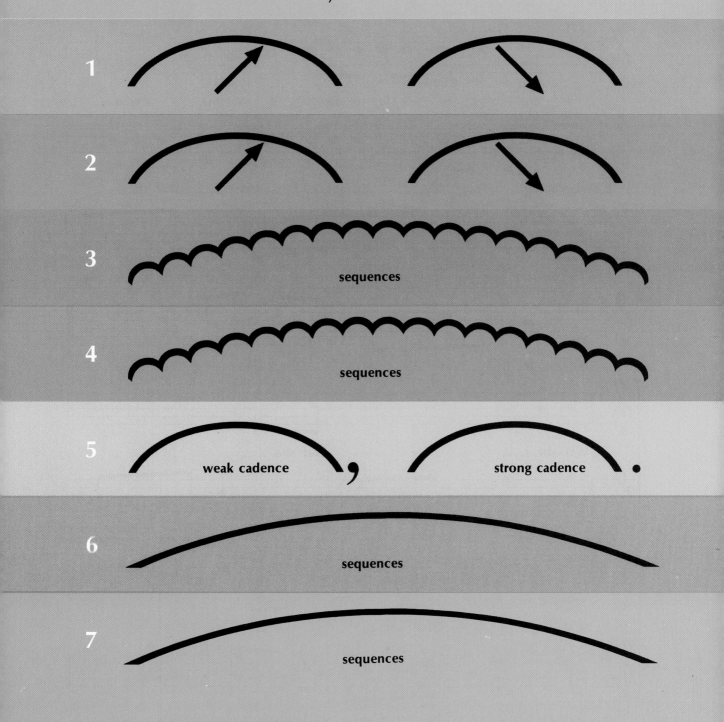

Sequences

In which section, A, B, or C, do you hear a melody pattern repeated at different pitch levels, called sequences?

TINA SINGU
FOLK SONG FROM AFRICA

FROM *CHANSONS DE NOTRE CHALET*.   COURTESY OF WORLD AROUND SONGS, BURNSVILLE, N.C.

Ti - na Sing - u, le - lu - vu - tae - o. Wat-sha,___ Wat-sha,___

Wat-sha.___ Wat-sha,___ Wat-sha,___ Wat-sha,___ Wat-sha,___

Wat-sha.___ La, la - la - la - la - la - la, la - la - la - la - la -

la, la - la - la - la - la - la - la - la - la - la.

Wat-sha,_____ Wat-sha,_____

La, la - la - la - la - la - la, la - la - la - la - la -

Wat - sha,_____ Wat - sha,_____ Wat - sha._____

la, la - la - la - la - la - la - la - la - la - la.

Listen to the recording. Each time a number is called, decide whether you hear sequences. If you do, choose the word *sequences*. If you do not, choose the words *no sequences*.

WHAT DO YOU HEAR? 5: Sequences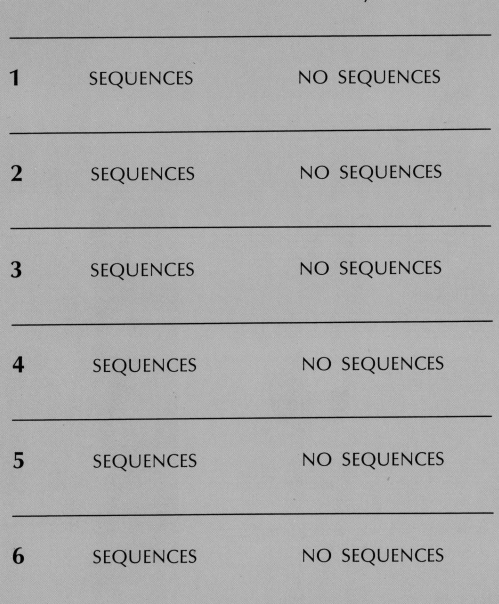

1	SEQUENCES	NO SEQUENCES
2	SEQUENCES	NO SEQUENCES
3	SEQUENCES	NO SEQUENCES
4	SEQUENCES	NO SEQUENCES
5	SEQUENCES	NO SEQUENCES
6	SEQUENCES	NO SEQUENCES

Intervals

The hands of a clock measure how time moves in *intervals*. The intervals of time are called seconds, minutes, and hours.

Notes on a staff measure how tones move in intervals. The intervals of music can be called *steps, leaps,* and *repeats.*

Listen to the Westminster chimes as they measure quarter-hour intervals. Can you hear and see the intervals between the tones?

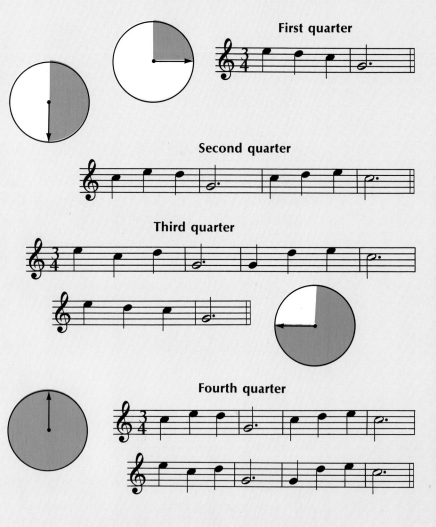

First quarter

Second quarter

Third quarter

Fourth quarter

Now toll the hour, using a low-C bell. What interval will you hear—steps, leaps, or repeats?

Melodies that Outline Chords

Play an F chord by strumming the strings of an Autoharp very slowly.

Listen to the different tones that make up an F chord—F, A, and C.

Find a part of the melody of this song that outlines the F chord.

In the same way, listen to the tones of the C₇ chord—C, E, G, and B♭. Find a part of the melody that outlines the C₇ chord.

LA CUCARACHA FOLK MELODY FROM MEXICO WORDS BY RICHARD EISMAN

1. There's a bug, some like to chase it, When we play we must out-race it,
2. Ti - ny thing with no *a - mi - gos,* Not a friend wher-ev-er it goes,
3. Let the bugs en - joy their free-dom, Ev - en though we do not need 'em,

If at lunch we see it com - ing, We're sup-posed to send it run-ning.
Do you real - ly want to ban - ish Lit - tle bugs who sing in Span - ish.
All *las ni - ñas* and *los ni - ños* Can't for - get their true *a - mi - gos.*

La cu - ca - ra - cha, I'm so sad to see you go,

La cu - ca - ra - cha, la cu - ca - ra - cha, I'm so sad to see you go.

La cu - ca - ra - cha, I love you; *te quie - ro yo.*

La cu - ca - ra - cha, la cu - ca - ra - cha, I love you; *te quie - ro yo.*

For a recorder ensemble, see p. 218. For a dance, see p. 246.

Melodies Based on Chords

This melody is based on chords in the C family—C, G_7, and F.

Where does the melody outline each chord?

MATILDA
FOLK SONG FROM JAMAICA

Ma - til - da, _____ Ma - til - da, _____

Ma - til - da, she take me mon - ey and run Ven - e - zue - la. _____

1. Five thou - sand dol - lars, friend, I

lost. The wo - man e - ven take me cart and horse. _____

Ma - til - da, she take me mon - ey and run Ven - e - zue - la. _____

2. My money was to buy me house and land,
   The woman she got a serious plan.
   Matilda, she take me money and run Venezuela.
   Refrain

3. Now the money was safe in me bed,
   Stuck in the pillow beneath me head,
   But Matilda, she find me money and run Venezuela.
   Refrain

4. Never will I love again,
   All me money gone in vain
   'Cause Matilda, she take me money and run Venezuela.
   Refrain

For a percussion ensemble, see p. 235.

This melody is based on chords in the G family—
G, D$_7$, and C.

Where does the melody use tones in each chord?

THE LORD IS MY SHEPHERD BLACK SPIRITUAL

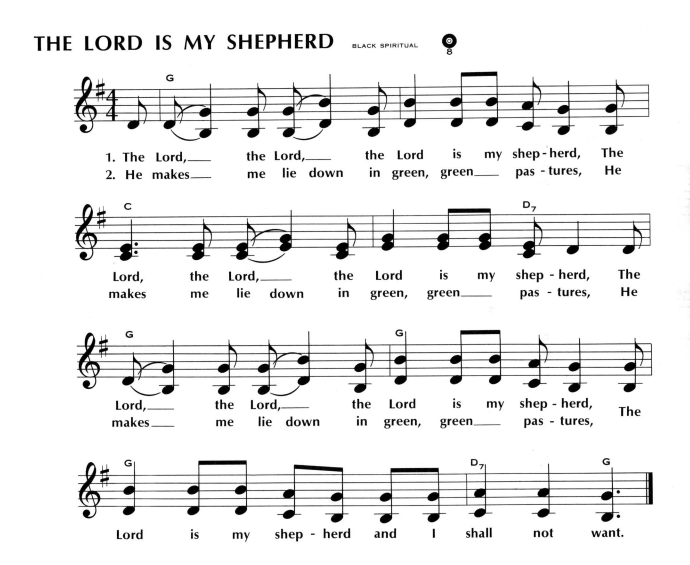

1. The Lord,___ the Lord,___ the Lord is my shep-herd, The
2. He makes___ me lie down in green, green___ pas-tures, He

Lord, the Lord,___ the Lord is my shep-herd, The
makes me lie down in green, green___ pas-tures, He

Lord,___ the Lord,___ the Lord is my shep-herd, The
makes___ me lie down in green, green___ pas-tures,

Lord is my shep-herd and I shall not want.

3. He leads me beside the still, still waters, (*3 times*)
   The Lord is my shepherd and I shall not want.

4. I'll fear no evil for Thou art with me, (*3 times*)
   The Lord is my shepherd and I shall not want.

For guitar fingerings, see p. 204.

More About Melody, Harmony, Texture 155

The Chromatic Scale

The melodies you sing, play, and listen to are made up of arrangements of tones, some of which are a half step apart and others a whole step apart.

To show half steps, line up all the bells from low C to high C.

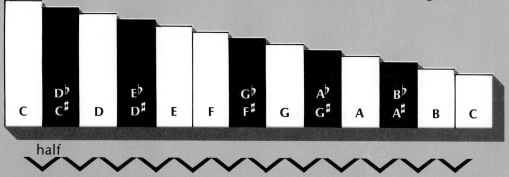

This is called the *chromatic scale*. To hear its general sound, play the bells upward, then downward. Play single tones and clusters of tones.

Here is a melody that is based on part of the chromatic scale.

Select the bells shown and try to play the melody with the recording while others sing.

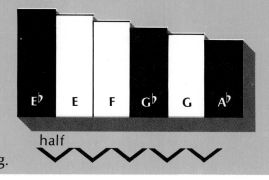

A SONG WITH NO KEY   WORDS AND MUSIC BY DAVID EDDLEMAN

Not too fast   *mp*

How can there be a song with no

key? It's hard to see how it can be.

Lis - ten to me and you will a - gree

There is no key. Oh, me.

The Whole-Tone Scale

Using the whole chromatic scale, change the half steps to whole steps by removing every second bell.

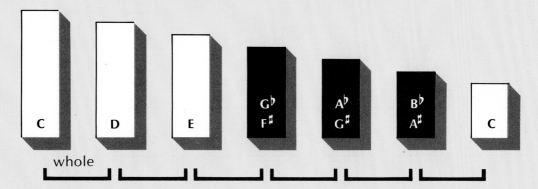

This is called the *whole-tone scale*. To hear the general sound, play the scale upward, then downward. Play single tones and clusters of tones.

This melody is based on a whole-tone scale. Sing or play it with the recording.

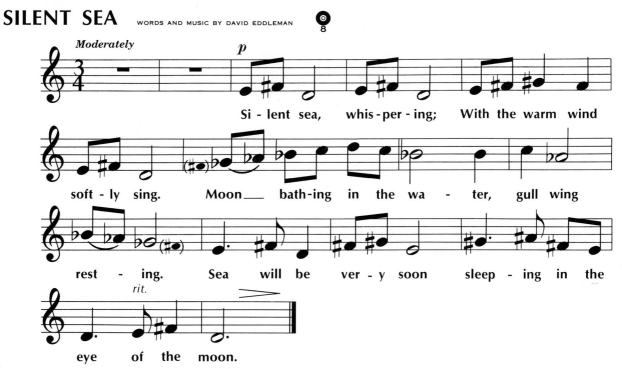

CALL CHART 10: Chromatic Scale, Whole-Tone Scale 🔊

Follow the chart to hear some pieces that make use of the chromatic and whole-tone scales.

1.	CHROMATIC	**4.**	CHROMATIC
2.	WHOLE-TONE	**5.**	CHROMATIC
3.	CHROMATIC	**6.**	WHOLE-TONE

The Major Scale

Many melodies you know are based on an arrangement of whole and half steps called a *major scale*.

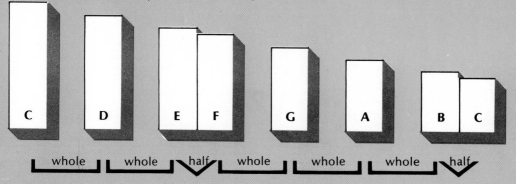

Play all the white keys or bells from low C to high C to hear the sound of the major scale in the key of C.

Now play "Jingle Bells" by ear, starting on E.

Practice building major scales in other keys: low D to high D, low F to high F, low G to high G, etc. Remember to follow the pattern of whole and half steps. Your ear will tell you if you make a mistake. Play "Jingle Bells" in other keys, starting on the third degree of each scale.

The Minor Scale

Many melodies you know are based on another arrangement of whole and half steps called a *minor scale.*

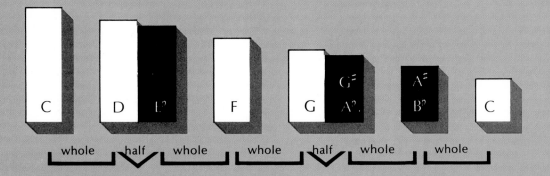

Line up the bells to build a natural minor scale from low C to high C.

Now change the tonality of "Jingle Bells" to minor. Play the melody starting on E^b.

Try building a minor scale from low E to high E. Remember to follow the pattern of whole and half steps shown above.

Now play one of the songs you know in E minor: Hey, Ho, Nobody Home, 136; Toembäi, 10; Shalom, Chaverim, 89; Zum Gali Gali, 136.

Here is a piece that uses both major and minor scales. The chart will tell you when the melody is based on a major scale and when it is based on a minor scale.

CALL CHART 11: Major Scale, Minor Scale

1 MINOR	**4** MAJOR
2 MINOR	**5** MINOR
3 MINOR	**6** MAJOR

Major and Minor Tonality

One of these songs is in a major tonality (it is based on a major scale). The other is in a minor tonality (it is based on a minor scale). Listen to the recording to hear which is major and which is minor.

ROCK-A MY SOUL

BLACK SPIRITUAL   ARRANGED BY JAMES W. ROOKER

For guitar fingerings to play the refrain, see p. 204.

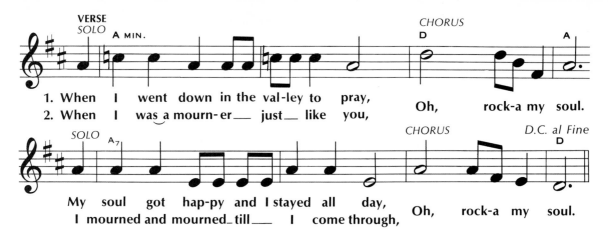

1. When I went down in the val-ley to pray, Oh, rock-a my soul.
2. When I was a mourn-er just like you,

My soul got hap-py and I stayed all day, Oh, rock-a my soul.
I mourned and mourned till I come through,

JOSHUA FOUGHT THE BATTLE OF JERICHO
BLACK SPIRITUAL

1-3. Josh-ua fought the bat-tle of Jer-i-cho, Jer-i-cho,

Jer-i-cho, Josh-ua fought the bat-tle of

Jer-i-cho, And the walls came tum-bling down!

1. You may talk a-bout your king of Gid-e-on, You may
2. Then up to the walls of Jer-i-cho He
3. Then the lamb, ram, sheep-horn be-gan to blow, And the

talk a-bout your man of Saul, There's none like good old
marched with a spear in hand, "go blow those ram horns,"
trum-pets be-gan to sound, Then Josh-ua com-mand-ed the

Josh-u-a At the bat-tle of Jer-i-cho.
Josh-ua cried,"'Cause the bat-tle is in my hand."
chil-dren to shout, And the walls came tum-bling down.

The Pentatonic Scale

Most melodies you know are based on a major scale or a minor scale. But some melodies are based on a five-tone scale, called *pentatonic*.

To build a G pentatonic scale, start on G and follow this pattern. One of the intervals is a step and a half.

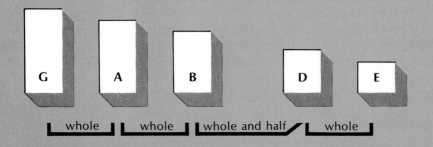

Here is a song based on the G pentatonic scale. To play it, you will need low D and E as well as high D and E.

After lining up the bells you need, try playing the melody as others sing.

WATERBOUND   TRADITIONAL

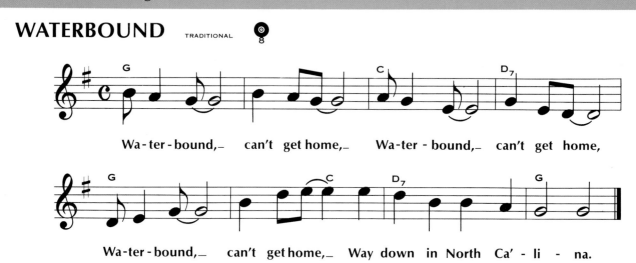

Wa-ter-bound,_ can't get home,_ Wa-ter-bound,_ can't get home,

Wa-ter-bound,_ can't get home,_ Way down in North Ca'-li - na.

2. Chickens a-crowin' from
   an old plough field, (*3 times*)
   Way down in North Ca'lina.

3. Nick and Charlie
   left to go home, (*3 times*)
   Before the water rises.

For guitar fingerings, see p. 204.

Analyze the intervals of the black keys of the piano.

What scale do they make?

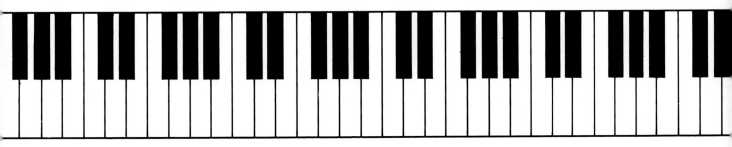

The sets of three and two black keys of the piano have the same arrangement of whole and half steps as this pentatonic scale. Play "Old Texas" by ear, starting on the lower key in the set of two black keys.

OLD TEXAS OKLAHOMA COWBOY SONG

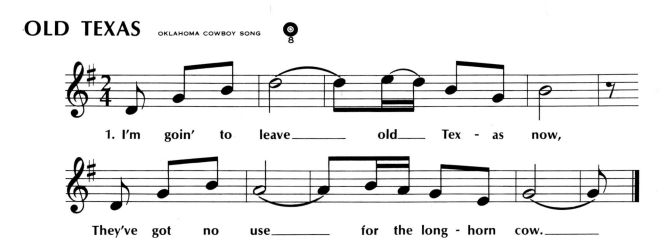

1. I'm goin' to leave_____ old___ Tex - as now,

They've got no use_____ for the long - horn cow._____

2. They've plowed and fenced my cattle range,
   And the people there are all so strange.

3. I'll take my horse, I'll take my rope,
   And hit the trail upon a lope.

4. Say *adios* to the Alamo
   And turn my head toward Mexico.

For a recorder ensemble, see p. 207.
For guitar fingerings, see p. 196.

Atonality

Many composers use all the tones within the octave as a basis for their music. The twelve tones are arranged in a certain order, called a *tone row*.

Each of the twelve tones in a tone row is just as important as all the others. Music based on a tone row is called *atonal*.

Before listening to a piece based on a tone row, arrange the bells so you can play it. Your performance will be part of the piece.

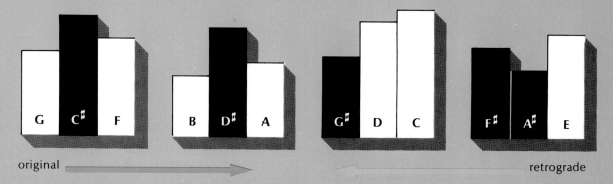

G C♯ F   B D♯ A   G♯ D C   F♯ A♯ E

original ──────────────▶   ◀────────────── retrograde

Group the tones in sets of three, as shown in the picture.

On this recording, you will hear string instruments play each set of three tones as a chord. Fill in the silence after each chord by playing the single tones in the set in any rhythm.

After this section, listen to the rest of the piece based on the same tone row.

At the end (coda), you play in the silences again. This time, play the single tones of each set from right to left (retrograde).

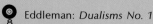 Eddleman: *Dualisms No. 1*

WHAT DO YOU HEAR? 6: Tonality

Listen to the recording. In the first three questions, you will be asked to decide whether the music you hear is tonal or atonal. In questions 4–6, you will be asked to hear whether the tonality stays the same or changes during the piece. In questions 7–9, decide whether the tonality is major or minor.

1	TONAL	ATONAL
2	TONAL	ATONAL
3	TONAL	ATONAL
4	TONALITY STAYS THE SAME	TONALITY CHANGES
5	TONALITY STAYS THE SAME	TONALITY CHANGES
6	TONALITY STAYS THE SAME	TONALITY CHANGES
7	MAJOR	MINOR
8	MAJOR	MINOR
9	MAJOR	MINOR

STYLE: MUSIC OF INDIA

When Western people think of Indian music,
they often think of the sitar, a guitar-like instrument
made popular by Ravi Shankar.

In India the sitar is used for playing classical music—
music improvised on very strict rules of melody (raga)
and time measure (tala).

In this example you will hear the sitar accompanied by a pair of drums, called *tabla*.

After a short section that has no definite rhythm, you will hear the drum play in a meter of 7. Keep time by clapping the beats that are marked with an X.

1	2	3	4	5	6	7
X			X		X	

While listening to Indian classical music, the audience keeps time by clapping and waving their hands. The first beat of the group of 7 is often shown with a wave of the hand or a clap with the back of the right hand on the palm of the left.

 Raga Yaman

In addition to Indian classical music, heard mostly in large cities, the country has a wealth of folk music enjoyed by the villagers. Small groups of musicians are hired to play "outdoor music" at weddings, births, and festivals.

Occupational songs are also commonly heard. Farmers sing as they work in the fields. Woodcutters have their special songs. Even workmen on a modern building will sometimes chant as they work.

Here is a folk song from the Sind region, where there is much fishing and trading along the coast. The women sing as they wait for the return of their loved ones, hoping they will bring money and jewels.

As you keep time by clapping, sing the refrain with the recording. *Ho jamalo* means "let us be together again."

🎵 *Ho Jamalo*

In this wedding song, the women of the Saora tribe are telling a young bride not to worry that she is leaving home.

🎵 *Saora Wedding Song*

How many different tones make up the melody?

Probably the earliest kind of music we know of in India are the religious chants, called the *Veda*. Composed by a tribe of nomadic shepherds, these hymns are sung without any musical instruments for accompaniment.

Listen to the way the singers ornament the melody line as they sing.

🎵 *Sama Vedic Chant*

This Hindu religious song tells of King Rama's first meeting with his wife, Sita. It is taken from a very old story of the adventures of King Rama.

Rama was a perfect king—so gentle, kind, and wonderful that the Indians now believe he must have been God disguised as a man.

🎵 *Song from the Ramayana*

This religious song is from the Muslim religion. Sing the repeated response "Allah hu," meaning "He is God," when you hear it on the recording.

🎵 *Allah hu*

You have heard several styles of Indian music—classical, folk, tribal, and religious. This is only a brief introduction to the great variety of music in India.

EXPERIENCING THE ARTS: PERCEIVING ART

When the arts reach us through our senses, our minds and our feelings get to work.

Our mind pulls together what our senses receive and organizes it. Not only do we see and hear. We notice, we are aware, we discover, we recognize, we remember, we understand. The word for all that is "perceive."

Our feelings are working at the same time. They are excited, aroused, stirred up, moved; we are involved, we are caught up, we respond. The word for all the things our feelings contribute is "react."

This formula shows the steps in the process of experiencing art.

SENSES	MIND	FEELINGS	EXPERIENCE OF ART
receive	perceives	react	

Van Gogh: THE STARRY NIGHT. Collection, The Museum of Modern Art, New York. Acquired through the Lillie P. Bliss Bequest.

SINGING IN CHORUS

PAVANE LOUIE L. WHITE

*Loo loo loo

loo loo loo loo loo, loo_____ loo, loo loo loo loo loo loo loo loo

loo loo loo_____

*or some neutral syllable

Loo   loo   loo   loo loo loo loo loo,   loo_____ loo,

loo loo loo loo loo loo loo loo loo _____ loo

Ah_____   ah_____

ah,_____   ah,_____

FASCINATING RHYTHM

MUSIC BY GEORGE GERSHWIN   WORDS BY IRA GERSHWIN   ARRANGED BY SOL BERKOWITZ

Fas - ci - nat - ing rhy - thm, you've got me on the go! Fas - ci -
once it did - n't mat - ter but now you're do - ing wrong; When you

Ah

nat - ing rhy - thm, I'm all a - quiv - er. What a mess you're mak - ing! The
start to pat - ter, I'm so un - hap - py. Won't you take a day off? De -

Ah

neigh - bors want to know why I'm al - ways shak - ing just like a fliv - ver.   Each morn - ing
cide to run a - long some - where far a - way off, and make it snap - py!

Ah   fliv - ver.   Each morn - ing
    snap - py!

I get up___ with the sun, Start a - hop - ping, nev - er stop - ping, To find at

I get up___ with the sun, Start a - hop - ping, nev - er stop - ping, To find at

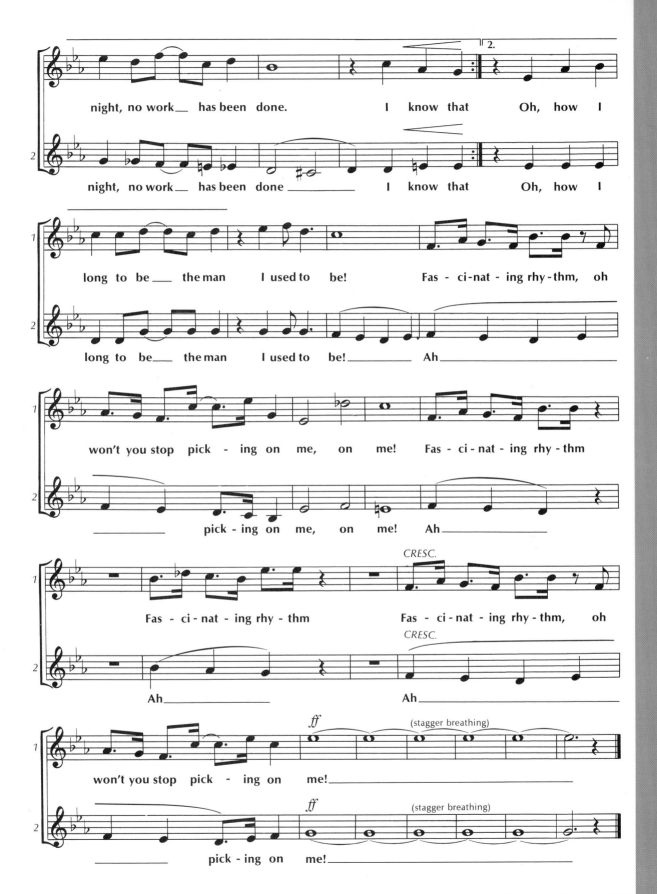

BLESS THE BEASTS AND CHILDREN

(FROM THE COLUMBIA PICTURES RELEASE: "BLESS THE BEASTS AND CHILDREN")

WORDS AND MUSIC BY BARRY DE VORZON AND PERRY BOTKIN, JR.   ARRANGED BY SOL BERKOWITZ.

Bless the beasts and the chil - dren,   for in this world they have no voice, _____ they have no choice. _____ voice, _____ Bless the beasts and the chil - dren, for the world can nev - er be, the world they see. _____ Light their way_

when the dark - ness ____ sur - rounds them; give them love,

let it shine all a - round ____ them. ____

Bless the beasts and the chil - dren; Give them shel -

- ter from the storm; ____ keep them safe; ____

keep them warm. ____ (close to hum)

LOOKS LIKE RAIN IN SUNNY LANE

WORDS AND MUSIC BY JIMMY CURTISS

1. Oh, you and I _____ lived in hous - es side by side _____ On a street _____ that bore the name _____ of Sun - ny Lane, _____ Sun - ny Lane. _____ We were hap - py there, _____ Had no wor - ries, had no cares; _____ Spent each day _____ dream - ing plans, _____ and plan - ning dreams, _____ think - ing schemes. _____

REFRAIN

1. Sun - ny Lane, Sun - ny, Sun - ny Lane. _____

MELODY

2. Now it looks like rain in Sun - ny Lane. _____

3. Now it looks like rain in Sun - ny, Sun - ny Lane. _____

at your emp - ty house___ stand-ing there,___ And it fills___

D.S. al Fine

___ my lone - ly heart___ with mem - o - ries___ of you and me.___

PRECIOUS STONES

MUSIC BY JOSEPH GOODMAN   WORDS BY CHRISTINA ROSSETTI

FROM SIX SONGS FOR CHILDREN'S CHORUS BY JOSEPH GOODMAN. COPYRIGHT 1973 GENERAL MUSIC PUBLISHING CO., INC. REPRINTED BY PERMISSION.

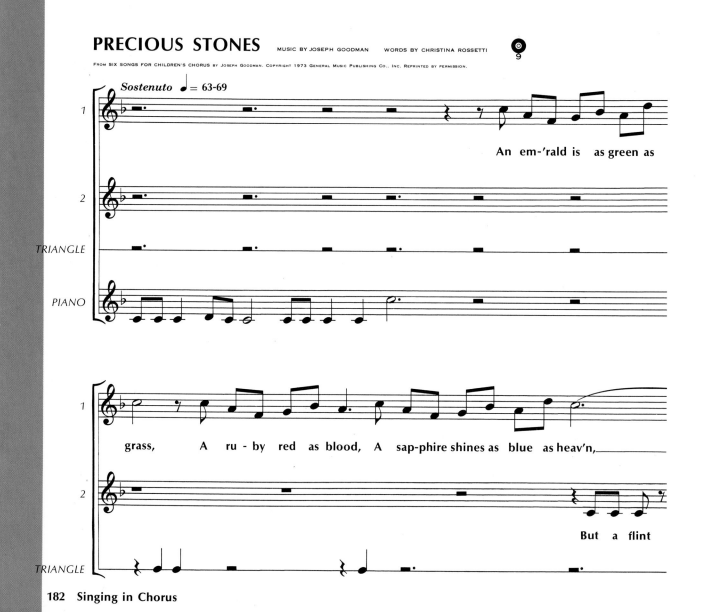

An em-'rald is as green as grass, A ru - by red as blood, A sap-phire shines as blue as heav'n,___

But a flint

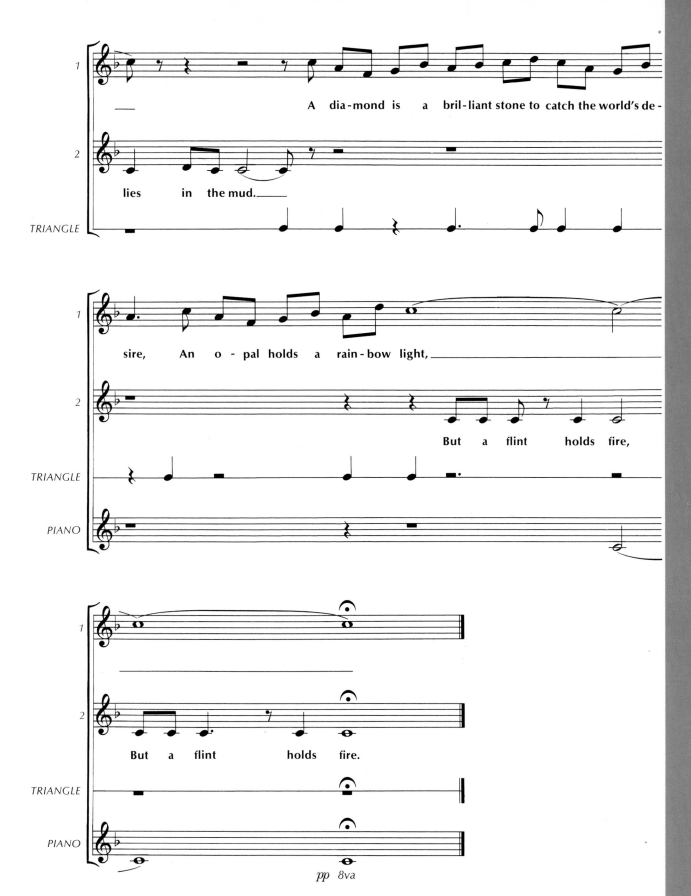

INFINITUDE DAVID EDDLEMAN

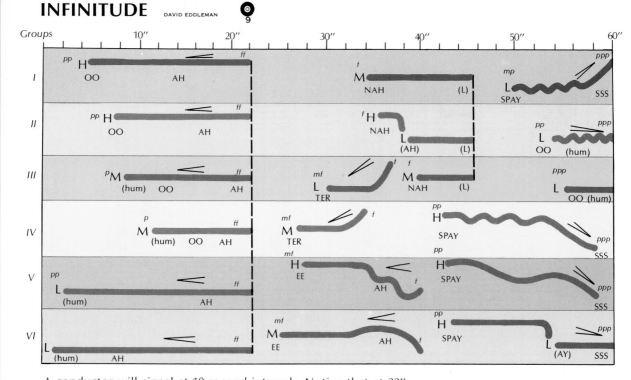

A conductor will signal at 10-second intervals. Notice that at 22″
(indicated by broken lines), there will be silence for about 2″ ■

At 24″, the words "eternal space" begin in group VI and are fragmented
among the other voices ■

Divide the chorus equally into six groups ■ Groups I and II are higher voices,
groups III and IV are medium voices, and groups V and VI are lower voices ■

For all groups: H any high note in *your* voice range ■ M any medium note
in *your* voice range ■ L any low note in *your* voice range

Each segment is about 10 seconds long ■ Timing is approximate ■

Syllables in capital letters indicate the sound you are to sing ■

Standard symbols are used for dynamic marks ■

After you are assigned to a part, read through it to get an idea of when
and how you are to sing ■

Directions for Performance of "CLEMENTINE"

The electronic music accompaniment for "Clementine" spoofingly
changes the pitch up and down at the points marked 〰 ■ Also,
the second verse is a half step higher than the first, and the third verse
is a half step higher than the second ■ Listen for your new pitch at the
start of each new verse ■ At the places marked 〰 try to follow
the sounds up and down with your voice, and be sure to return to the
right pitch for each verse, just as the accompaniment does ■ The line
above the vocal score indicates the accompaniment ■ Although the
score calls for the accompaniment and the chorus to begin at the same
time, the chorus can also begin at the second measure ■

CLEMENTINE

DORIS HAYS

FOR 2-PART CHORUS WITH ELECTRONIC SOUND ACCOMPANIMENT.   REALIZED AT QUEENS COLLEGE ELECTRONIC MUSIC STUDIO.

© 1973 DORIS HAYS

Clem - en - tine, Clem - en - tine, Clem - en - tine, Clem - en - tine, 2. Light she

1. In a
3. Drove she

cav - ern in a can - yon, Ex - ca - vat - ing for a mine, Dwelt a
was, and like a fair - y, And her shoes were num - ber nine, Her - ring
duck - lings to the wa - ter, Ev - 'ry morn - ing just at nine, Hit her

min - er, for - ty nin - er, And his daugh - ter Clem - en - tine.
box - es with - out top - ses, San - dles were for Clem - en - tine. Oh my
foot a - gainst a splin - ter, Fell in - to the foam - ing brine.

dar - lin', oh my dar - lin', Oh my dar - lin' Clem - en - tine, You are

CODA

lost and gone for - ev - er, dread - ful sor - ry Clem - en - tine.

Singing in Chorus 185

SIMPLE GIFTS

SHAKER HYMN   ARRANGED BY MARILYN DAVIDSON

'Tis the gift to be sim-ple, 'Tis the gift to be free, 'Tis the

'Tis the gift to be sim-ple, 'Tis the gift to

gift to come down where we ought to be, And when we find our-selves__ in the

come down where we ought to be, When we find__ our__

place just__ right, 'Twill__ be in the val - ley of love and de-light.

place just__ right, 'Twill be in love and de-light.

When true sim-plic - i - ty is gained, To bow and to bend we____

When true sim-plic-i-ty is gained, To bend we

shan't be a-shamed, To turn, turn will be our de-light, Till by

shan't be 'shamed, To___ turn___ will de-light, Till by

turn - ing, turn - ing we come round right.

turn - ing we come round right.

DONA NOBIS PACEM (*Give Us Peace*) TRADITIONAL ROUND

Do - na no - bis pa - cem, pa - cem, Do - na___

no - bis pa - cem. Do - na no - bis

pa - cem, Do - na no - bis pa - cem. Do - na

no - bis___ pa - cem, Do - na no - bis pa - cem.

ALL THROUGH THE NIGHT

WELSH AIR   VERSE 1 BY HAROLD BOULTON
VERSE 2 ATTRIBUTED TO THOMAS OLIPHANT   ARRANGED BY FRANZ JOSEPH HAYDN

VERSE 1 WORDS REPRINTED BY PERMISSION OF MESSRS. J. B. CRAMER & CO. LTD., LONDON

1. Sleep   my child, and peace   be with thee All   through the night;
2. While   the moon her watch   is keep - ing All   through the night;

Guard - ian an - gels God   will send thee All   through   the night.
While   the wea - ry world   is sleep - ing All   through   the night.

Soft   the drow - sy hours   are creep - ing, Hill   and   vale   in slum - ber steep - ing,
O'er   thy spir - it   gent - ly steal - ing, Vi - sions of   de - light re - veal - ing,

I   my lov - ing   vig - il keep - ing All through the night.
Breathes   a pure and   ho - ly feel - ing All through the night.

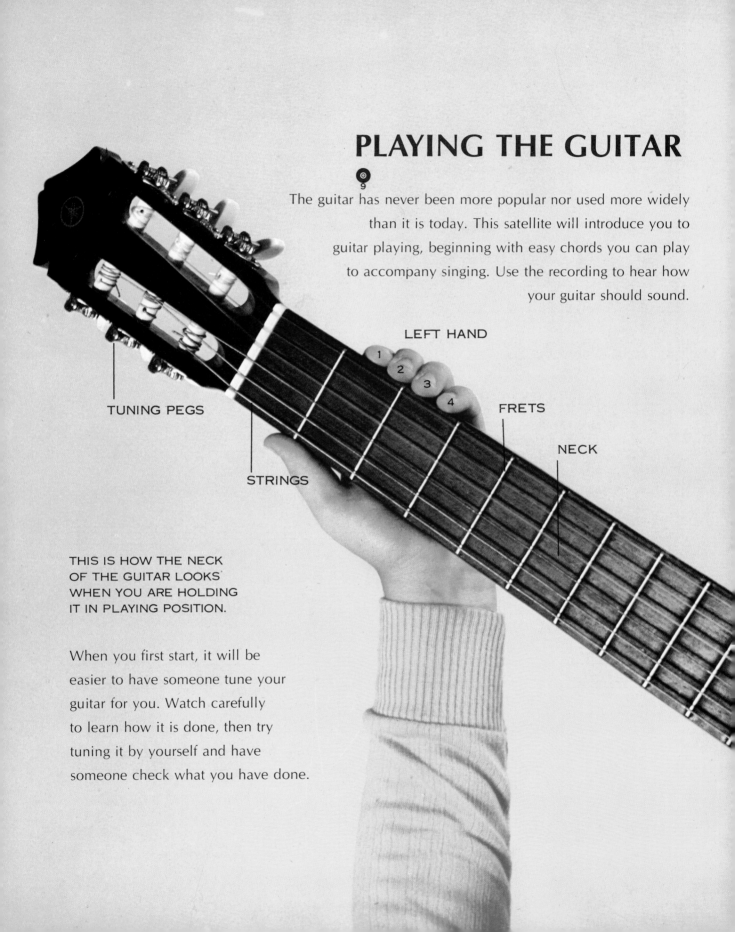

PLAYING THE GUITAR

The guitar has never been more popular nor used more widely than it is today. This satellite will introduce you to guitar playing, beginning with easy chords you can play to accompany singing. Use the recording to hear how your guitar should sound.

LEFT HAND

1
2
3
4

TUNING PEGS

FRETS

NECK

STRINGS

THIS IS HOW THE NECK OF THE GUITAR LOOKS WHEN YOU ARE HOLDING IT IN PLAYING POSITION.

When you first start, it will be easier to have someone tune your guitar for you. Watch carefully to learn how it is done, then try tuning it by yourself and have someone check what you have done.

THE E MINOR CHORD

A drawing of the top of the guitar's neck is used to show where to put your fingers on the strings. Compare the drawing with the photograph.

In this satellite, only the strings shown in red on the diagram are to be strummed. In the E Minor chord, all six strings are strummed.

When you are ready, play these three songs. Strum with the thumb of your right hand each time a small stroke (/) appears over the music.

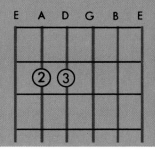

SHALOM, CHAVERIM   ISRAELI ROUND

E MIN.

Sha - lom, cha - ver - im! Sha - lom cha - ver - im! sha - lom, sha - lom. Le -
hit - ra - ot, le - hit - ra - ot, sha - lom,_____ sha - lom.

HEY, HO! NOBODY HOME   OLD ENGLISH ROUND

E MIN.

Hey,   ho!   No - bo - dy home. Meat   nor   drink   nor   mon - ey have I none,
Yet   I will   be mer - ry.___ Hey,   ho!   No - bo - dy home.

Another song you can play using only the E Minor chord is "Zum Gali Gali," *Silver Burdett Music 5*, p. 136.

Make up your own pattern of strumming for this song. Rap lightly on the body of the guitar instead of playing chords each time you sing the words *Jane, Jane*.

JANE, JANE
AMERICAN FOLK SONG   REPRINTED FROM SING OUT!—THE FOLK SONG MAGAZINE. USED WITH PERMISSION.

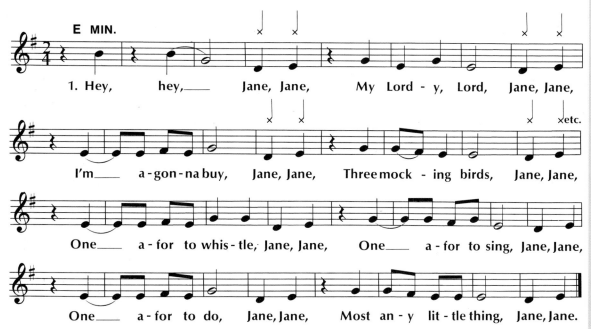

1. Hey,   hey,___   Jane, Jane,   My Lord-y, Lord,   Jane, Jane,
I'm___ a-gon-na buy,   Jane, Jane,   Three mock-ing birds,   Jane, Jane,
One___ a-for to whis-tle, Jane, Jane,   One___ a-for to sing, Jane, Jane,
One___ a-for to do,   Jane, Jane,   Most an-y lit-tle thing, Jane, Jane.

2. Hey, hey, Jane, Jane,
   My Lordy, Lord, Jane, Jane,
   I'm a-gonna buy, Jane, Jane,
   Three hunting dogs, Jane, Jane,
   One a-for to run, Jane, Jane,
   One a-for to shout, Jane, Jane,
   One to talk to, Jane, Jane,
   When I go out, Jane, Jane.

3. Hey, hey, . . .
   My Lordy, Lord, . . .
   I'm a-gonna buy, . . .
   Three muley cows, . . .
   One a-for to milk, . . .
   One to plough my corn, . . .
   One a-for to pray, . . .
   One Christmas morn, . . .

4. Hey, hey, . . .
   My Lordy, Lord, . . .
   I'm a-gonna buy, . . .
   Three little blue birds, . . .
   One a-for to weep, . . .
   One a-for to mourn, . . .
   One a-for to grieve, . . .
   When I am gone, . . .

THE C CHORD

To play the C chord, put finger 1, your index finger, on the B string, first fret. Strum the strings shown in red.

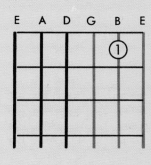

To play the G_7 chord, place finger 1 on the high E string, first fret, and strum the strings shown in red.

When you can play the G_7 chord, practice changing from C to G_7 and back until you can do it easily. Then you are ready to play this song. Notice that the chord changes each time you sing the word *money*.

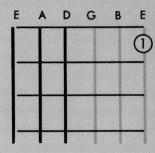

PAY ME MY MONEY DOWN
SLAVE SONG FROM THE GEORGIA SEA ISLANDS COLLECTED AND ADAPTED BY LYDIA A. PARRISH

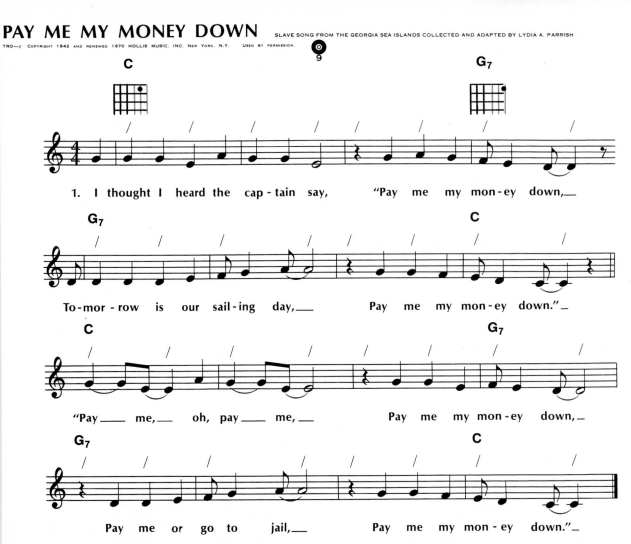

1. I thought I heard the cap-tain say, "Pay me my mon-ey down,—

To-mor-row is our sail-ing day,— Pay me my mon-ey down."—

"Pay — me,— oh, pay — me, — Pay me my mon-ey down,—

Pay me or go to jail,— Pay me my mon-ey down."—

2. As soon as the boat was clear of the bar,
    "Pay me my money down,"
    He knocked me down with the end of a spar,
    "Pay me my money down." *Refrain*

3. Well, I wish I was Mr. Steven's son,
    "Pay me my money down,"
    Sit on the bank and watch the work done,
    "Pay me my money down." *Refrain*

INTRODUCING THE BASS GUITAR

When you can play the song to accompany singing, or to accompany the recording, team up with a friend to play these parts for two guitars. The player who strums the chords is called the "lead" guitar. Another player, who plays only single tones on the low-sounding strings, is called the "bass."

Bass Guitar: Finger the E and A strings as shown. These will not be chords! The bass guitar player plays single tones only.

When the chord is C, alternate the A and E strings in each measure. You are playing the tones C and G.

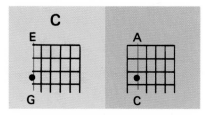

When the chord is G_7, alternate the E and D strings in each measure. You are playing the tones G and D.

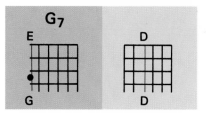

Here is a guitar part you can play to accompany the singing of a familiar song. Lead guitar plays chords in the rhythm shown or one the player chooses. Bass guitar plays single tones.

HE'S GOT THE WHOLE WORLD IN HIS HANDS BLACK SPIRITUAL

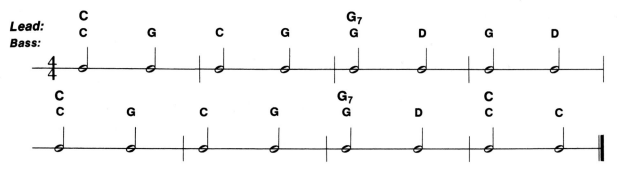

Team up with a friend. One of you plays the lead guitar part while the other plays the bass guitar part.

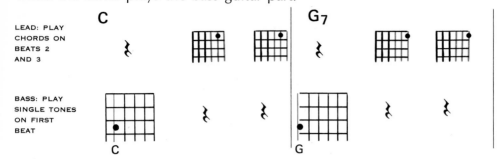

STREETS OF LAREDO AMERICAN COWBOY SONG

1. As I _____ walked out in the streets of La - re - do, As I walked
2. We'll play the drum slow - ly and play the fife low - ly, We'll play the

out in La - re - do one day, I spied a young cow - boy wrapped
dead march as we bear him a - long. We'll go to the grave - yard and

up in white lin - en, wrapped up in white lin - en as cold as the clay.
lay the sod o'er him; He was a young cow - boy but he had done wrong.

Lead guitar: Try varying the rhythm. Strum down with the thumb and up with the fingers

Bass guitar: For variety, play the tone for each chord on the first and third beats of each measure.

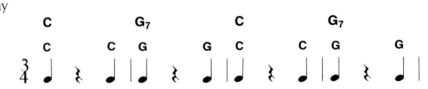

When changing from the G₇ to the C chord, play the tone D on the third beat just before the C chord.

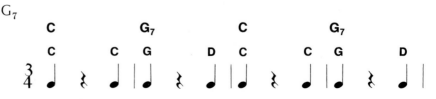

Here is another song using the C and G₇ chords.

Lead guitar: ♩ ♩ | *Bass guitar:* (C) (G₇) — C G D G

BUFFALO GALS   AMERICAN FOLK SONG

1. As I was walk-ing down the street, down the street, down the street, A
2. I asked her if she'd stop and talk, stop and talk, stop and talk, Her

pret-ty lit-tle girl I chanced to meet, un-der the sil-very moon._____
feet_ took_ up the whole side-walk, she was_ fair to view._____

Buf-fa-lo gals won't you come out to-night, come out to-night, come out to-night?

Buf-fa-lo gals won't you come out to-night and dance by the light of the moon?___

Lead guitar: 2/4 | *Bass guitar:* 2/4 (C) (G₇) — C G D G

SKIP TO MY LOU   AMERICAN GAME SONG

1. Flies in the butter-milk, shoo, fly, shoo!   Flies in the butter-milk, shoo, fly, shoo!
2. Little red wag-on paint-ed blue,   Little red wag-on paint-ed blue,

Flies in the butter-milk, shoo, fly, shoo!
Little red wag-on paint-ed blue,   Skip to my Lou, my dar-ling.

3. Lost my partner, what'll I do? . . .   4. I'll get another, better than you! . . .

THE G CHORD

Look at the diagram to figure out how to play a simple G chord. The photograph will help you.

Strum the strings shown in red. You can also include the D string in the chord for a fuller sound.

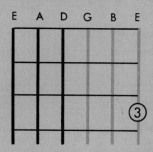

THE D₇ CHORD

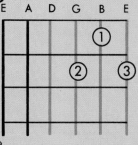

Here is the diagram showing how to finger the D₇ chord. Strum the strings shown in red. You can also include the A string in the chord for a fuller sound.

Try changing back and forth between D₇ and G. When you can make the change as smoothly as possible, try the following songs with the recording.

Bass guitar: Try to always play the root of the chord (G for the G chord; D for the D₇ chord) on the first beat when the chord changes.

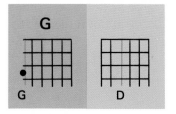

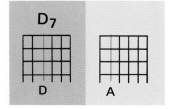

DOWN IN THE VALLEY
KENTUCKY FOLK SONG

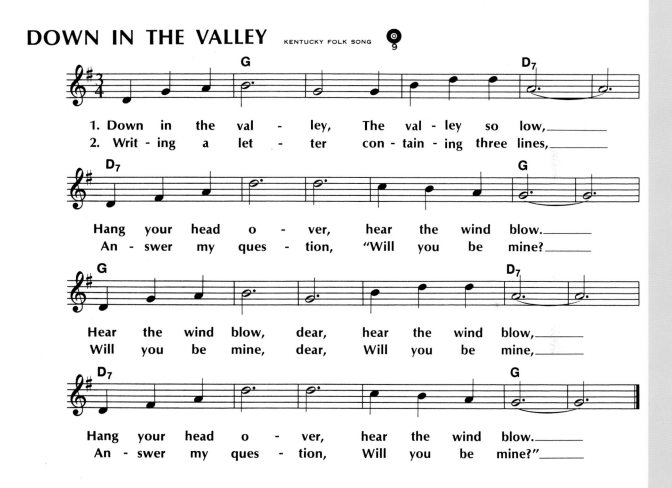

1. Down in the val - ley, The val - ley so low,_____
2. Writ - ing a let - ter con - tain - ing three lines,_____

Hang your head o - ver, hear the wind blow._____
An - swer my ques - tion, "Will you be mine?_____

Hear the wind blow, dear, hear the wind blow,_____
Will you be mine, dear, Will you be mine,_____

Hang your head o - ver, hear the wind blow._____
An - swer my ques - tion, Will you be mine?"_____

CLEMENTINE
AMERICAN FOLK SONG

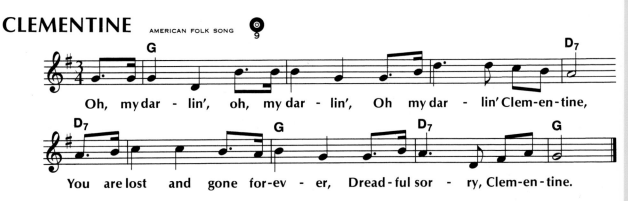

Oh, my dar - lin', oh, my dar - lin', Oh my dar - lin' Clem-en-tine,

You are lost and gone for-ev - er, Dread - ful sor - ry, Clem-en-tine.

Playing the Guitar 197

Here is another song to help you to practice the G and D_7 chords.

When the bass and lead guitars can accompany the singing,

add handclaps, tambourine, or other percussion to the performance.

OH, WON'T YOU SIT DOWN? BLACK SPIRITUAL

2. Who's that yonder dressed in blue?

   Must be the children that are comin' through.

   Who's that yonder dressed in black?

   Must be the hypocrites a-turnin' back. *Refrain*

PLAYING WITH THREE CHORDS

Many songs need at least three chords. With G, C, and D_7 (the G family) you can play a wide selection of songs.

Practice changing from one chord in the G family to another so you can accompany the next three songs.
Strum on each beat or make up a rhythm pattern of your own.

Bass guitar: Alternate the bass strings shown for each chord. Play on the strong beat of each measure. Remember, play the root (the note with the same name as the chord) on the first beat when the chord changes.

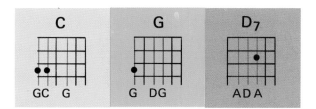

SHE'LL BE COMIN' ROUND THE MOUNTAIN
SOUTHERN MOUNTAIN SONG

1. She'll be com - in' round the moun - tain when she comes, She'll be

com - in' round the moun - tain when she comes, She'll be

com - in' round the moun-tain, She'll be com - in' round the moun-tain, She'll be

com - in' round the moun-tain when she comes.

2. She'll be drivin' six white horses when she comes, . . .
3. Oh, we'll kill the old red rooster when she comes, . . .
4. Oh, we'll all have chicken and dumplings when she comes, . . .
5. Oh, we'll all go out to meet her when she comes, . . .

LONESOME VALLEY
FOLK HYMN

You must walk___ that lone-some val-ley,___ You have to walk___
___ it by your-self,___ No-bo-dy else___ can walk it
for you,___ You have to walk___ it all a - lone.___

GET ON BOARD
BLACK SPIRITUAL

1. The gos - pel train is a - com - in',   I hear it close at
2. I hear the train a - com - in',   She's com - in' round the

hand,___   I hear the wheels a - rum - blin'   And
curve,___   She's loos - ened all her___ steam brakes   And

rol - lin' through the land.   Get on board, lit - tle
strain - in' ev - 'ry nerve.

chil - dren, Get on board, lit - tle chil - dren, Get on

board, lit - tle chil - dren, There's room for man - y - a more.

PLAYING WITH FOUR CHORDS

"Mama Don't 'Low" uses the chords G, D₇, G₇, and C. Listen to
the recording to see how the chords fit the music. After you have learned
"Mama Don't 'Low," you can add a bass guitar part played by a friend.

Bass guitar: Alternate the bass
strings shown for each chord.

Lead guitar: Vary the rhythm of
your strumming. Choose one of
these rhythms.

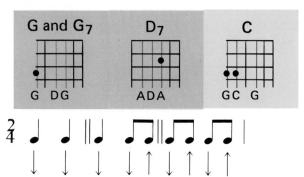

MAMA DON'T 'LOW   AMERICAN FOLK SONG

1.
2. } Ma - ma don't 'low no { gui - tar play - in' round here, _____
3. }   { ban - jo pick - in' round here, _____
                             { rock song sing - in' round here, _____

Ma - ma don't 'low no { gui - tar play - in' round here, _____
                        { ban - jo pick - in' round here, _____
                        { rock song sing - in' round here, _____

I don't care what Ma - ma don't 'low, Gon-na { play my gui - tar an - y - how,
                                               { pick my ban - jo an - y - how,
                                               { sing my rock songs an - y - how,

Ma - ma don't 'low no { gui - tar play - in' round here. _____
                        { ban - jo pick - in' round here. _____
                        { rock song sing - in' round here. _____

The D CHORD

Listen to the sound of the D chord
on the recording, then try it yourself.

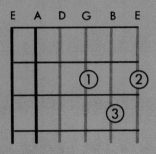

THE A₇ CHORD

The A₇ chord uses all six
strings. To change from the
D chord to the A₇ chord,
lift fingers 1 and 2 of your
left hand and move them
one string toward you,
staying in the second fret.

Bass guitar: Alternate the
bass strings shown for
each chord.

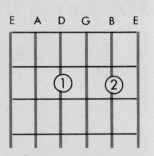

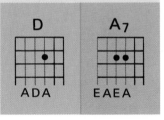

TOM DOOLEY   AMERICAN FOLK SONG

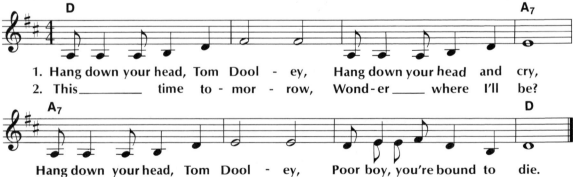

1. Hang down your head, Tom Dool - ey, Hang down your head and cry,
2. This_____ time to - mor - row, Wond - er _____ where I'll be?

Hang down your head, Tom Dool - ey, Poor boy, you're bound to die.
Down in some lone - some val - ley Hang-in' from a white oak tree.

Here is a four-chord song using D and A₇.

WHEN THE SAINTS GO MARCHING IN BLACK SPIRITUAL

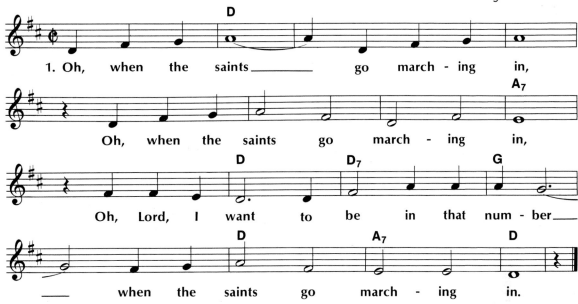

1. Oh, when the saints_____ go march - ing in,

Oh, when the saints go march - ing in,

Oh, Lord, I want to be in that num - ber_____

_____ when the saints go march - ing in.

2. Oh, when the stars refuse to shine, . . .   **3. Oh, when I hear that trumpet sound, . . .**

Using the chords you have learned in this satellite, you can play these songs in *Silver Burdett Music 5*.

CHORD CHART

Here are all the chords you have learned in this satellite. The strings to be strummed are shown in red. Bass guitar notes are shown at the bottom of this page.

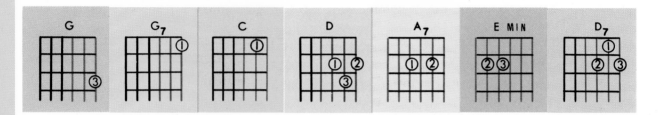

The fingerings you learned for G, G₇, and C are simplified fingerings. Here are the complete chords.

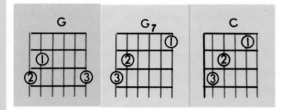

BASS GUITAR

The four strings of a bass guitar are tuned to the same pitches as the four lowest-sounding strings of a six-string guitar. These diagrams show all the <u>single tones</u> that you can choose to play for each chord shown.

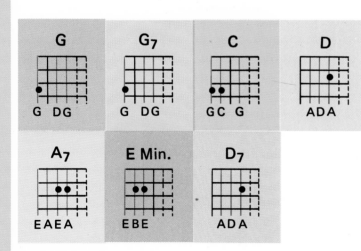

Note: These diagrams show some additional possibilities.

PLAYING THE RECORDER

This satellite will help you learn to play the soprano and alto recorders by yourself and with others. Both recorders use the same set of fingerings, but for different pitches.

Hold the recorder with both hands, as pictured. Make sure your left hand is above your right.

Cover-The Hole Test

Press just hard enough so that the hole will make a light mark on each finger and on the thumb of your left hand.

Making a Sound

Cover the tip of the mouthpiece with your lips. Your teeth should not touch the recorder.

Alto Recorder

Blow gently through the recorder, starting to blow with a "daah."

Private Practice

Soprano Recorder

Now you are ready to work with the fingerings. A diagram of the holes is used to show where to place your fingers to play the pitch. Each hole is covered by one specific finger and no other.

Experiment with each new pitch until your fingers feel secure. Play rhythm patterns of songs you know or improvise (make up) your own.

Three Notes to Begin

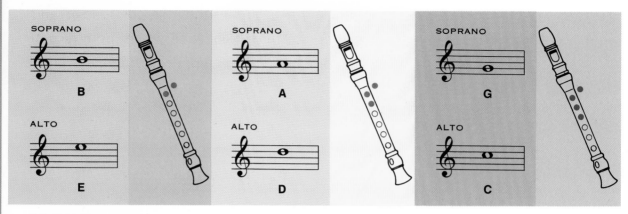

PRIVATE PRACTICE

Play the notes B, A, and G on the soprano recorder,

        E, D, and C on the alto recorder.

Then try these three-note melodies. First, listen to the recording.
Follow the score and finger the notes without playing. Then play
the melody by yourself or with the recording.

HOT CROSS BUNS

CHONG CHONG NAI   MALAYSIAN FOLK TUNE   © 1974 OXFORD UNIVERSITY PRESS

First Ensembles

Ensemble playing means playing in a group, carefully fitting
different parts together to make musical sense. When playing in
ensembles, you must listen to the other parts as you play.

MAMA DON'T 'LOW (Song on page 4)

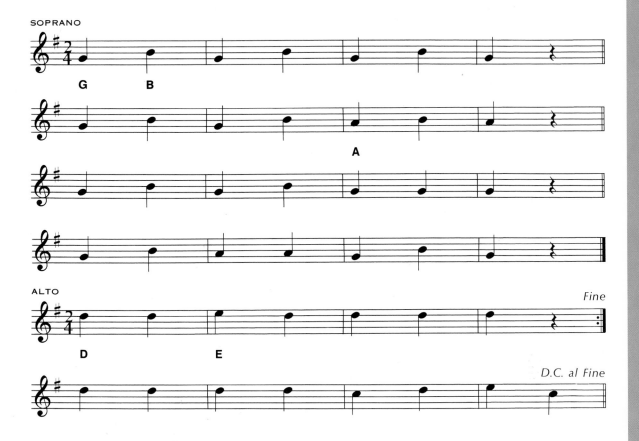

OLD TEXAS (Song on page 163)

For a larger ensemble, ask someone to play an Autoharp or guitar
accompaniment. Ask others to sing.

Two New Notes

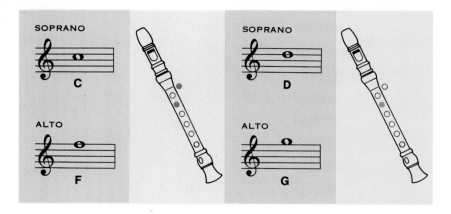

Private Practice

Now you can play five tones. Practice them and try the next two melodies.
Play your part while others sing the song and play chords on an Autoharp.

JINGLE BELLS

LADY, COME

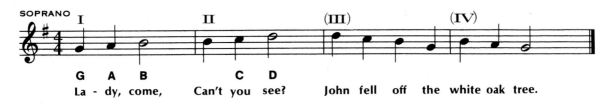

La - dy, come,   Can't you see?   John fell off   the white oak tree.

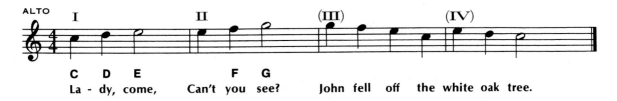

La - dy, come,   Can't you see?   John fell off   the white oak tree.

When you play the melody alone, try it as a round.

Choose others to play with you.

More Ensembles

ON TOP OF OLD SMOKY (Song on p. 64)

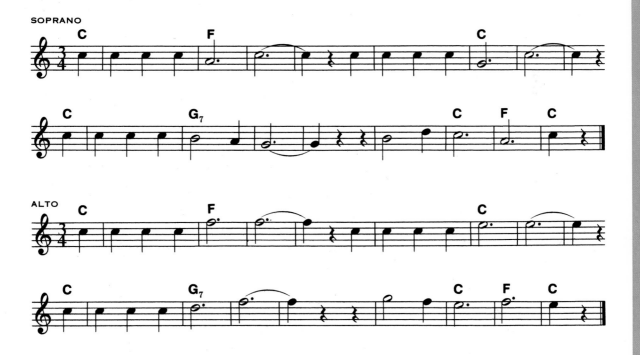

For a larger ensemble ask someone to play an Autoharp or guitar
accompaniment. Ask others to sing.

PAY ME MY MONEY DOWN (Song on p. 70)

Practice this part to play while others sing.

WHEN THE SAINTS GO MARCHING IN

Practice the melody on a soprano recorder.

Ask someone to play the countermelody on the alto recorder.

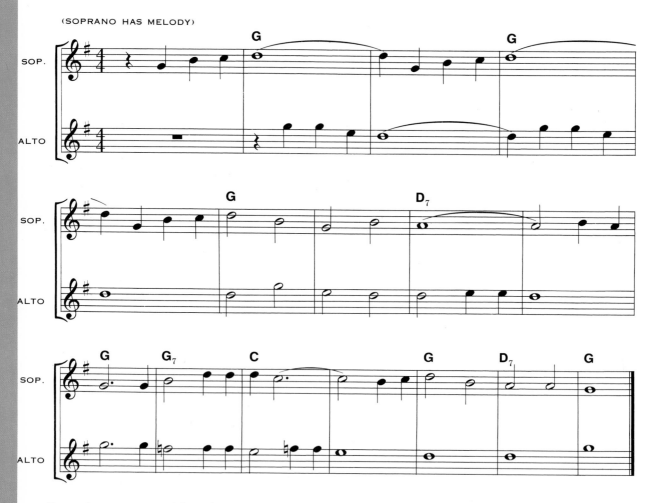

For a larger ensemble ask someone to play an Autoharp or guitar accompaniment. Ask others to sing.

PAY ME MY MONEY DOWN (Song on p. 70)

Practice this part to play while others sing.

For a larger ensemble ask someone to play the soprano part on p. 6.

Add an Autoharp or guitar accompaniment.

WHEN THE SAINTS GO MARCHING IN

Practice the melody on an alto recorder.

Ask someone to play the countermelody on a soprano recorder.

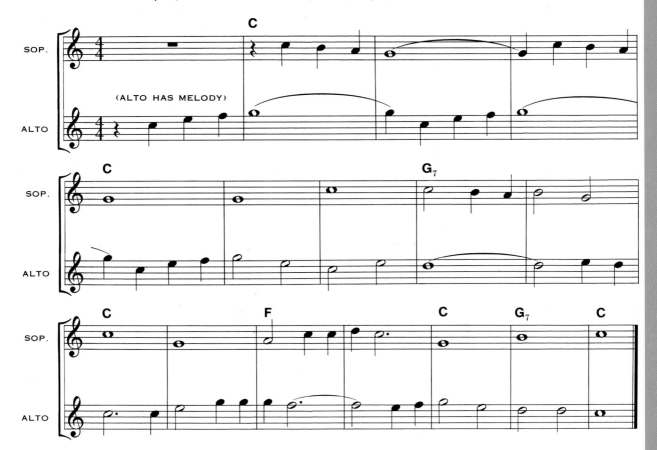

For a larger ensemble ask someone to play an Autoharp

accompaniment. Ask others to sing.

Two More New Notes

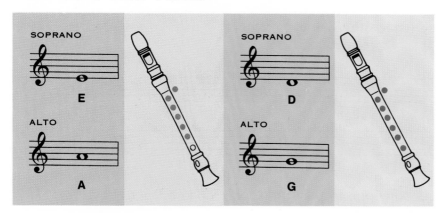

Private Practice

FISHPOLE SONG

This melody uses notes you know on the soprano recorder.

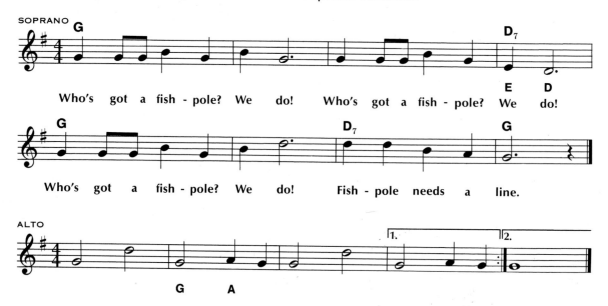

For a larger ensemble add Autoharp or guitar accompaniment while others sing.

Try This

While others sing, play this part on soprano and alto recorders each time it comes in the song "Jane, Jane." (The song is found in the Playing the Guitar satellite, page 191.)

Private Practice

FISHPOLE SONG

This melody uses notes you know on the alto recorder.

Who's got a fish-pole? We do! Who's got a fish-pole? We do!

Who's got a fish-pole? We do! Fish-pole needs a line.

Choose someone to play the soprano recorder with you.

For a larger ensemble add Autoharp or guitar accompaniment while others sing.

MORNING BELLS

This round uses notes you know on the soprano recorder. Play it
alone and as a round with others.

More Ensembles

Add the tone color of an alto recorder to the ensemble.

Add the tone color of a triangle to the ensemble. Play on the
first beat of every measure.

Private Practice

OH, WON'T YOU SIT DOWN?

Try playing the melody on p. 198 in the Playing the Guitar
satellite. It uses these notes on the soprano recorder.

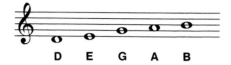

D E G A B

Ensemble

Here are two countermelodies that can be played with the
melody, one for soprano recorder, the other for alto recorder.

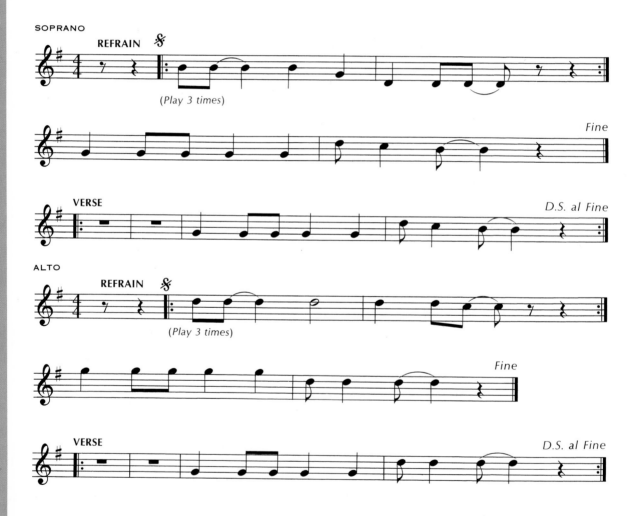

Put as many parts together as you can: voices, recorders, guitar, Autoharp.
Add hand claps, tambourine, and other percussion instruments to the performance.

Another New Note

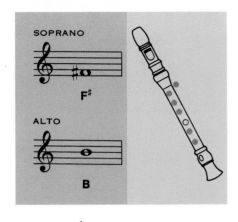

Private Practice

This repeated pattern, called an **ostinato,** uses a new note, F#. Practice it on the soprano recorder.

G F# E D

Use the ostinato when another soprano recorder plays "Fishpole Song" on p. 8 and "Oh, Won't You Sit Down," Playing the Guitar satellite, p. 198.

Practice this ostinato on an alto recorder. It uses a new note, B.

C B A G

Ask someone who plays the alto recorder to play "Fishpole Song" on p. 213 while you play the ostinato.

Ensemble

After you can play this melody, team up with two, three, or four friends who play the soprano recorder. Play the melody through at least two times. Then play it as a round. Parts II, III, and IV follow in turn two measures apart.

RECORDER SOUND PIECE 1: NOTES AND RHYTHMS

1. Copy the staff (5 lines and 4 spaces) as shown at the bottom
of the page. Be sure to include the bar lines, which show measures.

2. Lightly draw a pitch for each measure. Use the pitches in the
first column if you play soprano recorder, the pitches in the second
column if you play alto recorder. Pitches can be used more than once.

3. Using the pitch you have selected, fill in each measure with a rhythm
pattern from the third column. Each pattern may be used more than once.

4. Play your melody.

5. For an ensemble, team up with someone who has made up a melody on
either a soprano or alto recorder. Play the melodies alone, one after the
other (A B form). Then change the texture by playing both melodies together.

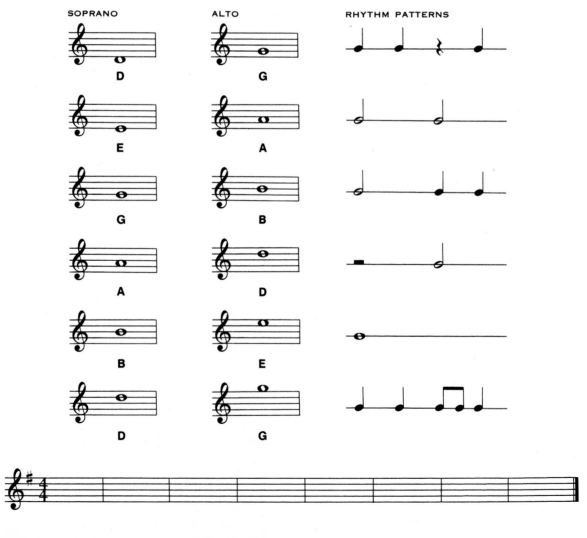

Private Practice for Soprano Recorder

Now that you know the fingering for F$^\sharp$, you can play the melodies of the following songs on the soprano recorder.

- Clementine, p. 197
- Down in the Valley, p. 197
- It's a Small World (Section B), p. 48
- Water Come a Me Eye, p. 84
- When the Saints Go Marching In, p. 203

Private Practice for Alto Recorder

For more practice using the new note, B, alto recorder players can play the melody of the following songs, reading from the soprano recorder scores.

- Hot Cross Buns, p. 206
- Chong Chong Nai, p. 206
- Jingle Bells, p. 208
- Lady Come, p. 209
- When the Saints Go Marching In, p. 210

Ensembles for Alto Recorders

For an ensemble using only alto recorders, combine any of the parts on the following pages.

- Mama Don't 'Low, p. 207
- Old Texas, p. 207
- On Top of Old Smoky, p. 209
- Pay Me My Money Down, pp. 210, 211
- When the Saints Go Marching In, pp. 210, 211

Add Autoharp, guitar, or percussion instruments to the ensemble.

Another New Note

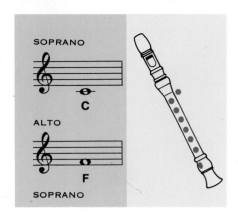

SOPRANO
C

ALTO
F

SOPRANO

Private Practice

Before playing this song, find the new note in the score for the recorder you play.

HOP UP AND JUMP UP

C   G   E   C

ALTO

F   C   A   F

Ensemble

For an ensemble, play your parts as others sing and dance. (See the Responding Through Movement satellite, p. 246.)

LA CUCARACHA

SOPRANO

ALTO

Another time, experiment with different rhythm patterns in 3 meter.

RECORDER SOUND PIECE 2: CREATING A MELODY

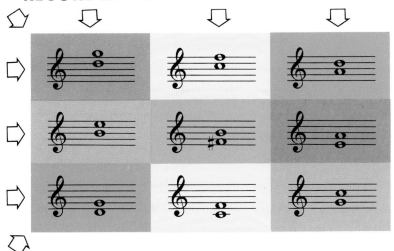

You know how to play nine tones on the recorder. Use these tones to make up your own melody.

Follow the arrows to play a sequence of notes in any order. The upper note on each staff is for alto recorder; the lower note for soprano.

When you have worked out a sequence of notes, add your own rhythm pattern for each box. Another time, change the meter. Play rhythm patterns in 3 meter, then in 2 meter.

Private Practice

THE BIRD'S SONG   ROUND FROM QUEBEC

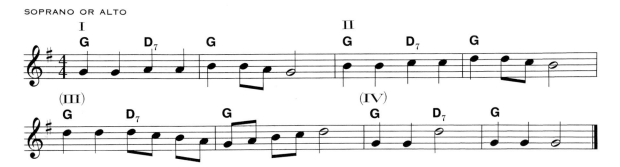

Ensemble

• Play melody as a two-part round on soprano recorder, alto recorder, or both. Then try playing it as a round in three or four parts.
• Add the Autoharp or guitar to the ensemble.
• Play melody while others add ostinatos below on recorders or bells.

Ensemble

While others sing, add one or more of these parts to the ensemble.

WATER COME A ME EYE (Song on p. 84)

You have now finished the Playing the Recorder satellite in Book 5.
Look for other pieces and songs to play on your recorder. You can continue
to learn more about recorder in the Playing the Recorder satellite in Book 6.

READING RHYTHM

BEAT

Have you ever heard a train's wheels as they "clack-clack-clacked" along the track? Or a wrist watch tick-tocking away? Or a leaky faucet going "drip-drip-drip?" You probably noticed the way the sounds repeated at exactly the same length of time. Maybe you tapped your foot or patted your knee in time with them.

What you heard and felt was a basic element of rhythm: *beat*. In music, the beat, also called the *pulse*, can be represented by a single note. Listen to the following beat pattern. Follow each beat, here represented by a *quarter note* (♩)

♩ ♩ ♩ ♩ ♩ ♩ ♩ ♩

In much of the music you sing there is a beat that goes on and on. If the music gets faster or slows down, it is because the beat gets faster or slows down.

Steady Beat; Quarter Notes

You can play each beat in the song "Mama Don't 'Low," page 4, while others sing or while you follow the recording. Play the beats on a woodblock while following this score. Notice that the beats are grouped in sets of two. The vertical lines are called *bars,* or *barlines,* and the distance between barlines is called a *measure.*

MAMA DON'T 'LOW   (See page 4.)

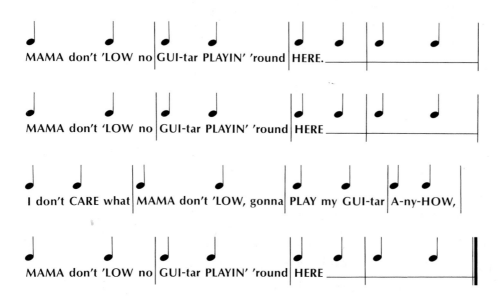

MAMA don't 'LOW no | GUI-tar PLAYIN' 'round | HERE. _____

MAMA don't 'LOW no | GUI-tar PLAYIN' 'round | HERE _____

I don't CARE what | MAMA don't 'LOW, gonna | PLAY my GUI-tar | A-ny-HOW,

MAMA don't 'LOW no | GUI-tar PLAYIN' 'round | HERE _____

Experiment with other ways to play beats to accompany "Mama Don't 'Low." For example, tap your toe on one beat and clap on the next beat.

TAP

CLAP

(⁊ IS A SYMBOL FOR ONE BEAT OF SILENCE.)

Half Notes

Team up with a friend. While you play every beat on a woodblock (two in each measure), your friend plays on a triangle a note that lasts for two beats—the entire measure.

The note that is being held through two beats is called a *half note* (♩). The length (duration) of this note is equal to two quarter notes when they are tied together (♩ = ♩♩). Here is a part for two players, to accompany "I'm Gonna Sing Out," page 24. One plays high and low temple blocks, or two woodblocks, the other a triangle. What notes are used in the score?

I'M GONNA SING OUT

2 TEMPLE BLOCKS OR WOODBLOCKS

Meter Signature

The *meter signature*—the numbers that appear at the beginning of a musical composition—tells you two things about the rhythm of the music. The top number tells *how many* beats are in each measure; the bottom number tells what note represents *one* beat.

2 = **2** BEATS IN EACH MEASURE
4 = A QUARTER NOTE REPRESENTS ONE BEAT

3 = **3** BEATS IN EACH MEASURE
4 = A QUARTER NOTE REPRESENTS ONE BEAT

4 = **4** BEATS IN EACH MEASURE   } CAN ALSO BE WRITTEN
4 = A QUARTER NOTE REPRESENTS ONE BEAT   } AS C (COMMON TIME)

Practice this part for gourd (or bongo) and guiro. Two players can accompany "Mineira de Minas," page 20, while others sing or as you listen to the recording. If stereo is available, use Pick-a-Track to hear how both rhythm patterns sound when played together. Be careful; this song begins in 3/4 and changes to 4/4.

MINEIRA DE MINAS (See page 42.)

Eighth Notes

You may already know that two eighth notes (♫ or ♪♪) are equal
to one quarter note (♫ = ♩). Listen to the following rhythm
pattern on the recording to hear how eighths and quarters fit together.

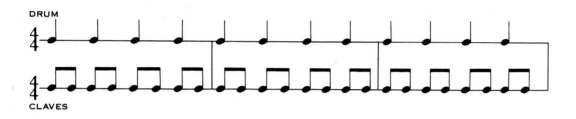

Now play the following part on claves. It uses both quarter
and eighth notes. After practicing the part, add it to the ensemble
on page 224 while others sing, or as you follow the recording.
Watch for the change to $\frac{4}{4}$ in the middle of the song.

THIRD PART TO
MINEIRA DE MINAS

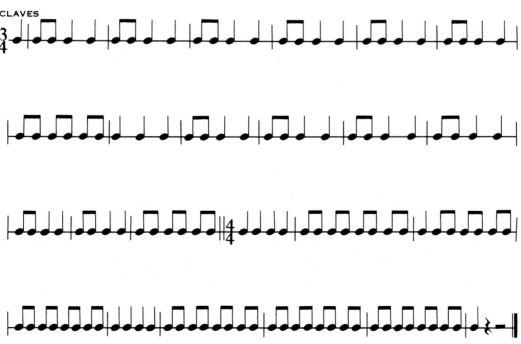

Triplets

In Mineira de Minas you played two eighth notes on one beat.
Sometimes three equal notes are played in the space of one beat.
These are called *triplets*. Triplets usually have a small 3 over the
notes: ♫. Speak the word "merrily" several times while clapping
a steady beat on the first syllable. You will be speaking triplets.

Listen to the recording to hear how triplets divide each beat into three
sounds. Which instrument plays the steady beat? Which plays triplets?

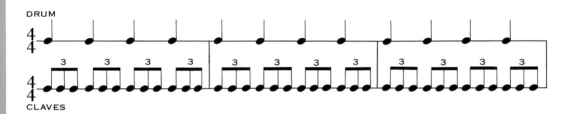

"Look Out!" by Doris Hays, is another song in which the meter changes,
but this time it changes in every measure, following this pattern:

| 2 beats | 3 beats | 4 beats |.

Practice this arrangement for triangle, finger cymbals, and temple blocks or
woodblock, to play with the song "Look Out!"

LOOK OUT   DORIS HAYS

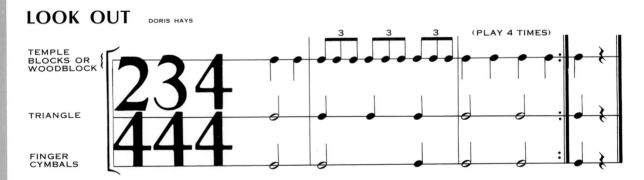

This part for "Pat-a-Pan," page 27, may be played on a drum using
your hands. Notice that each half note is notated ♪. The three slashes
through the stem indicate a *roll* (very fast hits) on the drum head for
the duration of the half note.

226   **Reading Rhythm**

PAT-A-PAN

Rests

Rhythm patterns are made of sounds
and silences. Just as there are symbols
for each duration of sound, there
are symbols for each duration
of silence, or rest.

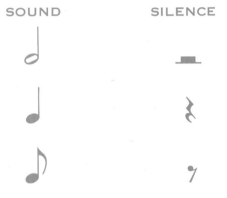

The following part uses both sounds and rests. Practice this part
to accompany the singing or playing of "Zigy, Zigy, Za," page 53.

ZIGY, ZIGY, ZA   (THE SYMBOL > TELLS YOU TO STRESS OR <u>ACCENT</u> THAT NOTE.)

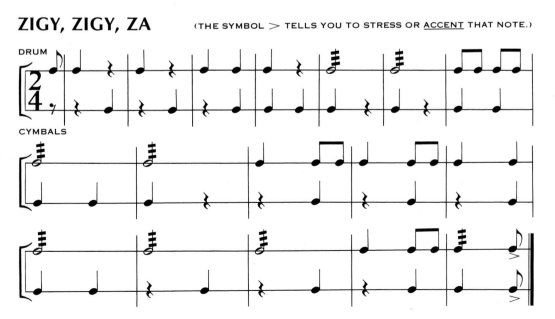

Try using what you know by playing rhythms on instruments. This ensemble, or group of instruments, can accompany the song "Tzena, Tzena," page 50. Each player in the ensemble selects one part to play. After practicing your part at home or in school, add it to another until all parts are playing. If you need help, listen to the recording.

TZENA, TZENA

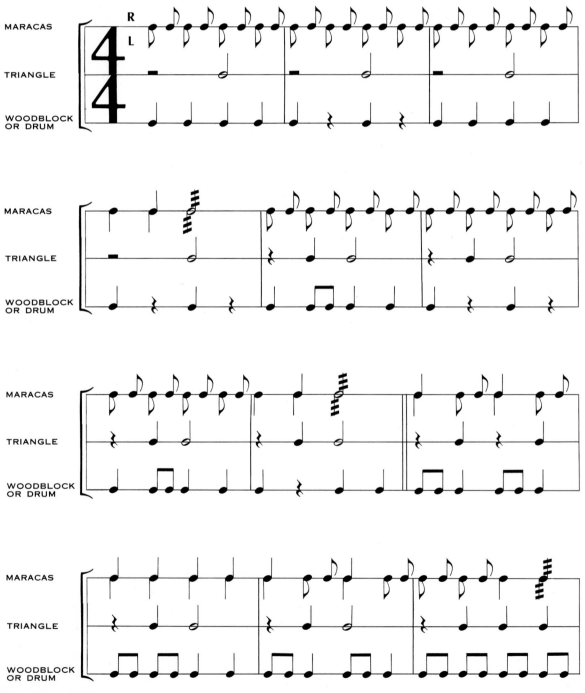

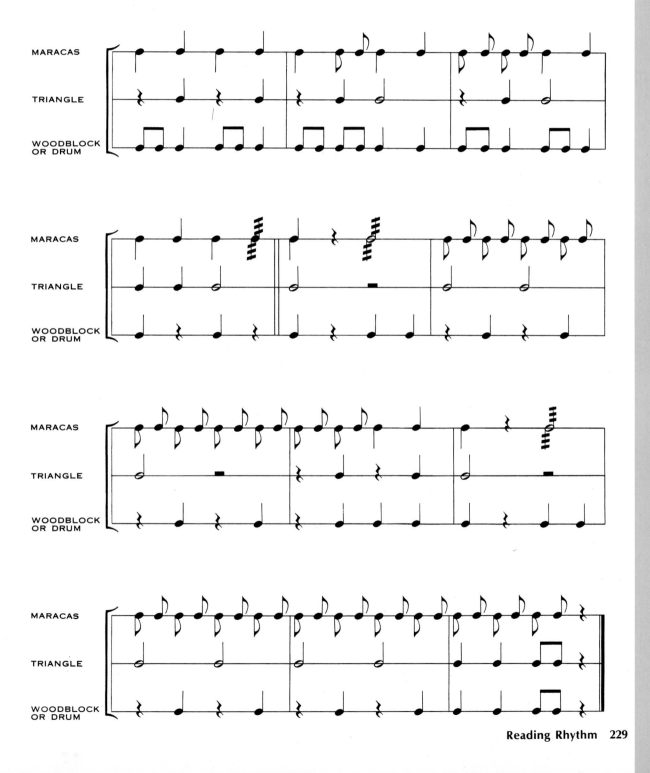

Sixteenth Notes

If you can divide by two you can understand the system used in notating rhythm patterns. Just as the half note (♩) can be divided into two quarter notes (♩ = ♩ ♩), and a quarter note into two eighth notes (♩ = ♫), so an eighth note can be divided into two sixteenths (♪ = ♪ ♪ or ♫). Listen to the recording to hear how sixteenths sound against half, quarter, and eighth notes.

The longest sound in the last measure is a *whole note* (o). Its sound lasts the whole measure. In the meter $\frac{4}{4}$, how many beats will this note last?

Look at this drum part for "Deep Blue Sea," page 66. What notations do you find? You should see $\frac{4}{4}$, $\frac{2}{4}$, ♩, 𝄾, 𝅘𝅥𝅯𝅘𝅥𝅯𝅘𝅥𝅯𝅘𝅥𝅯, 𝄿, | |, and >. If you know how to perform all these symbols in sound, practice the part to accompany the song. Be sure the sixteenth notes are played evenly—four sounds to one beat.

DEEP BLUE SEA   (See page 66.)

Here is an ensemble you and your friends can play to accompany "Thank God, I'm a Country Boy," page 68. Listen to the recording, then try it yourself. If stereo is available, use Pick-a-Track to hear how both rhythm patterns sound when played together.

THANK GOD, I'M A COUNTRY BOY

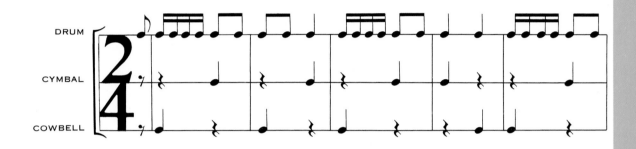

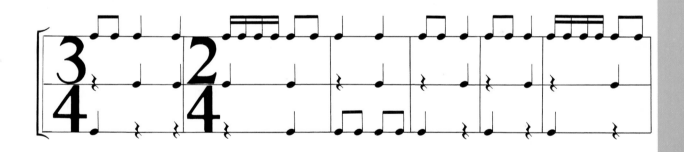

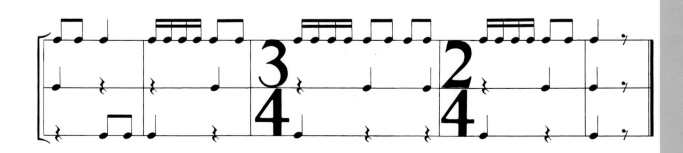

Dotted Rhythms

A dot after a note makes it longer by half its value. Look at the following table for an easy way to think of dotted rhythms.

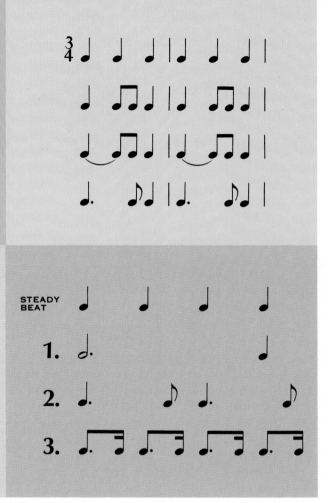

Do you notice that the dot takes the place of the tie? What would a dotted half (♩.) equal? What would a dotted quarter (♩.) equal? Listen to these patterns on the recording. First, you will hear the steady beat, then you will hear each pattern played three times.

The rhythm pattern in this ensemble to accompany *The Hammer Song,*" page 86, uses two of the dotted rhythms above, as well as quarter notes and quarter rests.

THE HAMMER SONG (See page 86.)

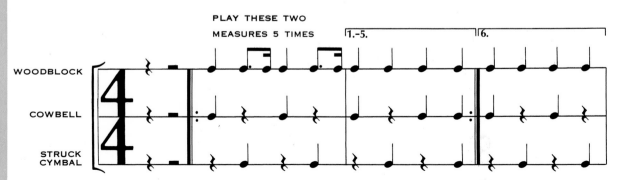

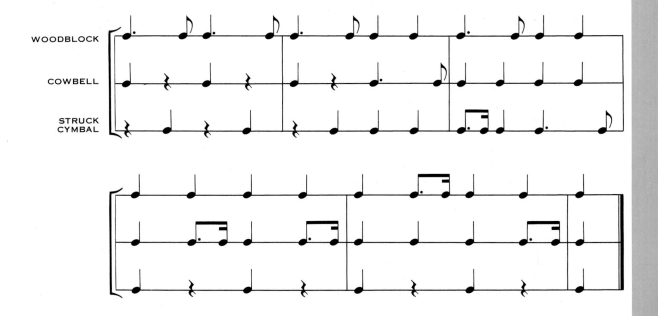

Try playing another accompaniment that uses dotted rhythms to play with "The Ocean Waves," page 129. Form an ensemble of instruments and singers to perform this piece.

THE OCEAN WAVES

Syncopation

Listen to the following pattern on the recording.

The pattern in the first half of each measure is called *syncopation*.
The special feeling of syncopation comes from playing a note on the weak part
of the beat and holding it through the strong beat. The syncopated notes
fall *between* the steady beats.

The following part played on a tambourine can accompany "Vine and Fig Tree,'"
page 137. Find the measures that use syncopation. Listen to the recording
to hear how the syncopation fits the steady beat, then try playing the part yourself.

VINE AND FIG TREE

TAMBOURINE

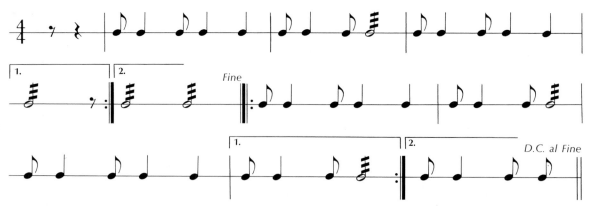

The next score also contains syncopation as well as other
rhythm patterns you have studied in this satellite.

MATILDA

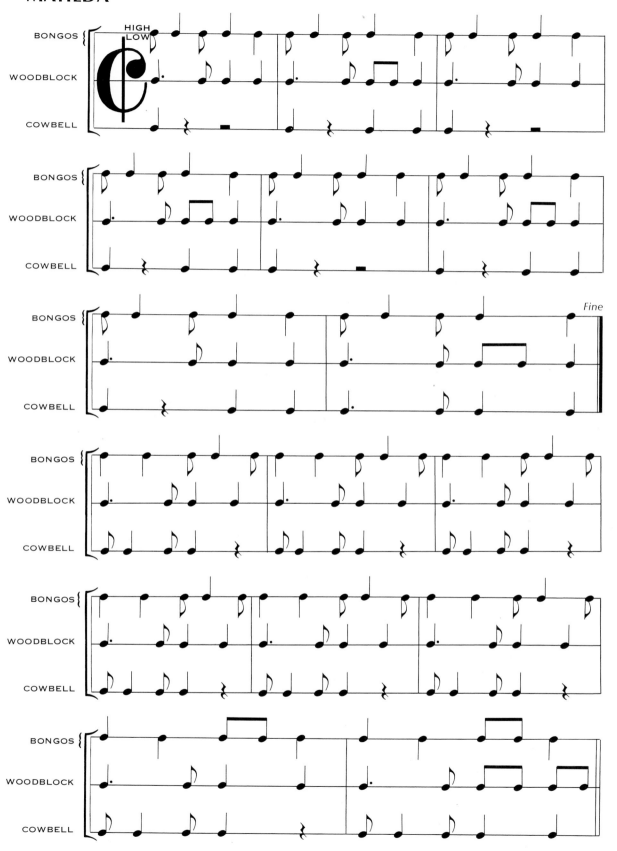

Review Ensemble

This rhythm ensemble contains all the rhythms
you have learned in this satellite.

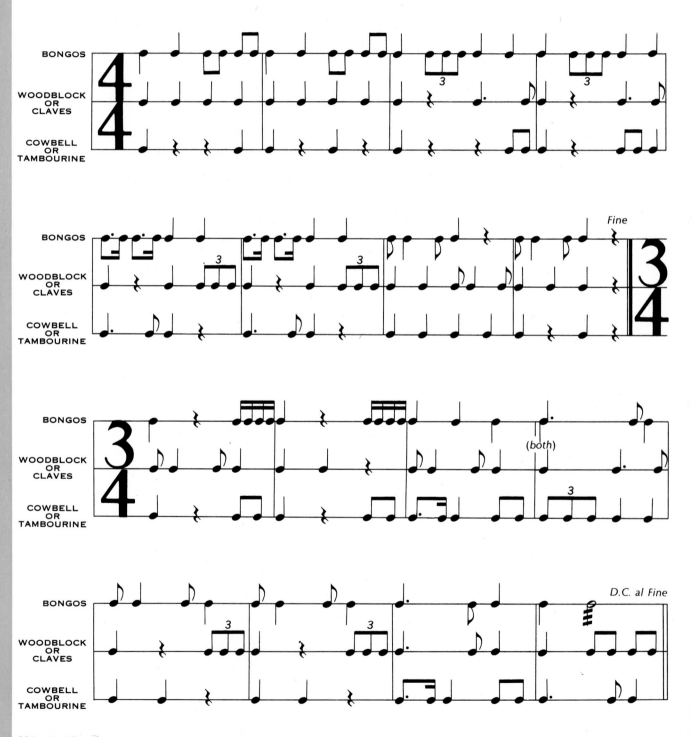

RESPONDING THROUGH MOVEMENT

INTRODUCTION
When you move to music you
respond to some of the same
qualities as when you sing
and play.

TEMPO

METER

STEADY BEAT

PHRASING

Organize a group to try some
of the movement suggestions
on these pages. Practice
at school or at home.

Dressing Up the Steady Beat

Pretend to play steady beats on a bongo drum; your hands will make the same movements over and over.

Now vary your movement by playing the steady beat on imaginary drumheads that are placed in different parts of the room—ceiling, floor, door, opposite walls, and so forth. To do this without moving your feet, you will need to reach, stretch, and bend—high and low, forward and backward, and diagonally. Although the steady beat remains the same, your movement can have many variations.

Plan a phrase in which one movement moves into another. How long will your phrase of movement be? How will you begin? How will you end? After you have decided, ask someone to accompany your movement on a percussion instrument.

Experiment further by adding accents to your movements; by changing the tempo to very fast or very slow.

Fancy Stepping to the Steady Beat

Keep time to the steady beat of *Shoeflies* by strutting on the first and third beats of each measure and adding a different movement on the second and fourth beats. You will find some suggestions for a fancy step at the right.

 Sakayama: *Shoeflies*

Now plan a phrase of movement that combines two or more fancy steps.

Using the Steady Beat in a Line Dance

After moving to the steady beat in *Shoeflies,* try this line dance with the same music. Find a place where you will have room to move backward, forward, and sideways.

PHRASE 1 (8 BEATS): WALK BACKWARD—RIGHT, LEFT, RIGHT. TOUCH FLOOR WITH LEFT FOOT.
WALK FORWARD—LEFT, RIGHT, LEFT. TOUCH FLOOR WITH RIGHT FOOT.

PHRASE 2 (8 BEATS): WALK SIDEWAYS AND STEP RIGHT, LEFT, RIGHT. TOUCH FLOOR WITH LEFT FOOT.
REPEAT TO THE LEFT—STEP LEFT, RIGHT, LEFT. TOUCH FLOOR WITH RIGHT FOOT.

PHRASE 3 (8 BEATS): STEP RIGHT, TOUCH LEFT NEXT TO RIGHT.
STEP LEFT, TOUCH RIGHT NEXT TO LEFT.
STEP RIGHT, TOUCH LEFT.
CLICK HEELS TWICE.

PHRASE 4 (8 BEATS): TAP FLOOR TWICE IN FRONT WITH RIGHT (2 BEATS).
TAP FLOOR TWICE IN BACK WITH RIGHT (2 BEATS).
TAP RIGHT FOOT ONCE FORWARD (1 BEAT), ONCE BACKWARD (1 BEAT), ONCE TO THE SIDE (1 BEAT).
PIVOT ON LEFT FOOT, MAKING A QUARTER TURN TO THE LEFT (1 BEAT). YOU ARE NOW FACING IN ANOTHER DIRECTION.

REPEAT FROM THE BEGINNING AS MANY TIMES AS DESIRED.

Block-Passing Game

Sometimes the steady beat changes tempo. It gets faster or slower. How does the tempo change in the music for the block-passing game on page 6 in your book?

 "Sasa akroma"

Children in Brazil play a variation of this block-passing game with the song "Zigy, Zigy, Za" (page 58). The game is played exactly like Block-Passing Game, with one exception.

When you come to the words *zigy, zigy, za,* keep the block in your hand as you pretend to put it down and pick up another one. Continue passing the block on the word *za.*

"Zigy, Zigy, Za"

Schottische: The Beat in 4's

The basic step of the schottische is in $\frac{4}{4}$ meter. Before planning a group dance, try the basic step and the variation with the recording.

Basic schottische step

STEP   STEP   STEP   HOP   STEP   STEP   STEP   HOP

Variation

STEP   HOP   STEP   HOP   STEP   HOP   STEP   HOP

 *Balkan Hills Schottische*

Now listen for the length of phrases in the music. Then try doing the basic step in different directions—forward, backward, diagonally, and around. Change direction for each new phrase.

Schottische Dance	
FORMATION:	PARTNERS STAND SIDE BY SIDE IN A CIRCLE, FACING COUNTERCLOCKWISE, AND WITH INSIDE HANDS JOINED.
PHRASE 1 (8 BEATS):	STARTING WITH OUTSIDE FOOT, TAKE TWO SCHOTTISCHE STEPS FORWARD.
PHRASE 2 (8 BEATS):	STARTING WITH OUTSIDE FOOT, TAKE TWO SCHOTTISCHE STEPS BACKWARD.
PHRASE 3 (8 BEATS):	TAKE ONE SCHOTTISCHE STEP SIDEWAYS, AWAY FROM YOUR PARTNER (4 BEATS). TAKE ONE SCHOTTISCHE STEP SIDEWAYS TOWARD YOUR PARTNER (4 BEATS).
PHRASE 4 (8 BEATS):	JOIN BOTH HANDS WITH YOUR PARTNER AND STEP-HOP (SCHOTTISCHE-STEP VARIATION) IN A CIRCLE IN PLACE, ENDING IN YOUR ORIGINAL POSITION, READY TO START THE DANCE AGAIN.

Polka: The Beat in 2's.

Before trying the polka step, keep time to the rhythm of the polka music on the recording by galloping around the room.

 Emilia Polka

Now try eight gallops with the right foot leading, followed by eight gallops with the left foot leading.

When you can change from right foot leading to left foot leading, try changing lead foot after every four gallops; after every two gallops. You are now doing the basic polka step, which has a feeling of a gallop.

Basic polka step

Try dancing the polka step to the music on the recording.

Two variations of the polka step

1. STAND SIDE BY SIDE WITH A PARTNER, INSIDE HANDS JOINED.

2. FACING A PARTNER, WITH BOTH HANDS ON EACH OTHER'S SHOULDERS, SLIDE TO THE LEFT DURING ONE PHRASE (8 SLIDES). SLIDE TO THE RIGHT DURING THE NEXT PHRASE (8 SLIDES).

Make up your own dance by adding a phrase or more of each variation to the basic polka step.

DAYENU

HEBREW PASSOVER SONG   ENGLISH WORDS BY ELIZABETH S. BACHMAN

10

1. He has led us out of E-gypt, led His peo-ple out of E-gypt,

He has led us out of E-gypt, da-ye-nu.

REFRAIN

Da - da - ye-nu,_____ da - da - ye-nu,_____

Da - da - ye-nu, da-ye-nu da-ye-nu da-ye-nu,

Da - da - ye-nu,_____ da - da - ye-nu,_____

Da - da - ye-nu, da-ye-nu da-ye-nu.

2. He has given us the Sabbath, given us the holy Sabbath,
   He has given us the Sabbath, *dayenu. Refrain*

3. He has given us the Torah, given us the blessed Torah,
   He has given us the Torah, *dayenu. Refrain*

Feel the beats in sets of four as you dance to the music of "Dayenu."

🎵 "Dayenu"
10

FORMATION: ANY NUMBER OF DANCERS STAND IN A CIRCLE (FACING THE CENTER) HOLDING JOINED HANDS AT SHOULDER LEVEL.

Section A (short phrases of 4 beats)

4 BEATS: STEP SIDEWAYS RIGHT, STEP LEFT IN BACK OF RIGHT, STEP RIGHT, STAMP LEFT.

4 BEATS: STEP SIDEWAYS LEFT, STEP RIGHT IN BACK OF LEFT, STEP LEFT, STAMP RIGHT.

4 BEATS: STEP FORWARD RIGHT, STAMP LEFT WHILE RAISING ARMS. STEP BACKWARD LEFT, STAMP RIGHT, LOWERING ARMS.

4 BEATS: STAMP RIGHT, LEFT, RIGHT, HOLD.

Section B (long phrases of 16 beats)

16 BEATS: WITH HANDS STILL JOINED, ALL TURN SLIGHTLY TO THE RIGHT AND DANCE 7 POLKA STEPS TO THE RIGHT, STARTING WITH RIGHT FOOT. (FOR BASIC POLKA STEP, SEE PAGE 241).
TO COMPLETE THE PHRASE, DROP HANDS, TURN AROUND TO THE RIGHT, AND QUICKLY JOIN HANDS AGAIN. THE CIRCLE IS NOW INSIDE OUT.

16 BEATS: DANCE 7 POLKA STEPS TO THE RIGHT, STARTING WITH THE RIGHT FOOT. TO COMPLETE THE PHRASE, DROP HANDS AND TURN RIGHT. THE CIRCLE IS NOW FACING CENTER AGAIN.

The Hora

FORMATION: ANY NUMBER OF DANCERS STAND IN A CIRCLE, FACING TOWARD THE CENTER. EACH PERSON PLACES A HAND ON THE SHOULDER OF THE PERSON ON EACH SIDE.

1. STEP SIDEWAYS WITH LEFT FOOT.
2. STEP ON RIGHT FOOT, PLACING IT BEHIND LEFT FOOT.
3. STEP ON LEFT FOOT.
4. HOP ON LEFT FOOT, SWINGING RIGHT LEG IN FRONT.
5. STEP ON RIGHT FOOT.
6. HOP ON RIGHT FOOT, SWINGING LEFT LEG IN FRONT.
(REPEAT)

Practice the hora with the recording of one of the songs you know:
"Tzena, tzena," page 50; "Toembaï," page 10; "Zum Gali Gali," page 136.

GREEK DANCE

In this New Year's dance from Greece, the eight-step dance
pattern matches the length of each phrase in the music.
Directions for the eight-step dance pattern are written under the
first phrase of the music.

NEW YEAR CAROL   (AS DANCED BY TULA LOMIS)   FOLK SONG FROM GREECE   ENGLISH WORDS BY STELLA PHREDOPOLOUS

Lift your voic - es, sing to - geth - er, wel - come the brand new year.

R = RIGHT FOOT STEP   CROSS L   STEP   CROSS L   STEP   POINT L   STEP POINT R
L = LEFT FOOT   RIGHT   IN BACK   RIGHT   IN FRONT   RIGHT   IN FRONT   LEFT IN BACK
                          OF R   OF R

In this time of hap - pi - ness, this time of good cheer

Ban - ish all your cares, for on this ho - ly feast_____

Saint Ba - sil comes bear - ing gifts of love and peace.

"New Year Carol"
10

Practice the dance pattern until you can
perform it in the tempo of the music.
Repeat the pattern throughout the dance.

For a group dance, any number of dancers
join hands in an "open" circle and
follow the leader.

Greek Dance in 3's: Tsamiko

Before trying the foot movements, listen for the tempo of the beat and play the rhythm pattern of this phrase on a percussion instrument. The pattern uses half notes and quarter notes.

Basic pattern

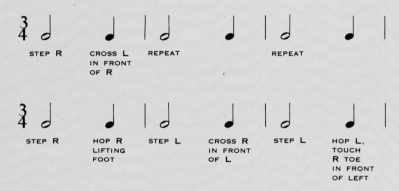

STEP R   CROSS L IN FRONT OF R   REPEAT   REPEAT

STEP R   HOP R LIFTING FOOT   STEP L   CROSS R IN FRONT OF L   STEP L   HOP L, TOUCH R TOE IN FRONT OF LEFT

Now do the foot pattern, following the basic rhythm pattern.

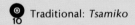 Traditional: *Tsamiko*
10

Try dancing in a group. With hands joined, form an open circle with a leader at one end. The leader, holding a handkerchief, moves the line about the room in snakelike fashion—weaving to the right, to the left, and so forth—while doing different tricks: leaping, dancing backward, and so on.

Mexican Dance in 3's: La Cucaracha

To feel the meter in 3, try this basic foot pattern. First practice it alone and then facing a partner.

Basic pattern

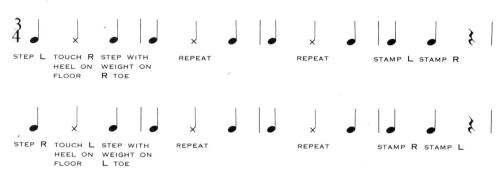

| STEP L | TOUCH R HEEL ON FLOOR | STEP WITH WEIGHT ON R TOE | REPEAT | REPEAT | STAMP L STAMP R |

| STEP R | TOUCH L HEEL ON FLOOR | STEP WITH WEIGHT ON L TOE | REPEAT | REPEAT | STAMP R STAMP L |

When you can do the basic foot pattern, practice it with the music.

 "La Cucaracha"

Now, try doing a waltz-walk. Think "down, up, up."

Waltz-walk

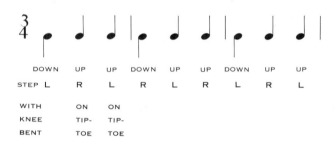

DOWN	UP	UP	DOWN	UP	UP	DOWN	UP	UP
STEP L	R	L	R	L	R	L	R	L
WITH KNEE BENT	ON TIP-TOE	ON TIP-TOE						

When you can do the basic foot pattern and the waltz-walk, you are ready to use them in a dance.

FORMATION:	ANY NUMBER OF PARTNERS, FACING EACH OTHER IN A SINGLE CIRCLE.
SECTION A:	DANCE THE BASIC FOOT PATTERN.
SECTION B:	PARTNERS STILL FACING, EACH DANCER WALTZ-WALKS FORWARD AROUND THE CIRCLE, PASSING RIGHT SHOULDERS.
	AT THE END (CADENCE) OF SECTION B, DANCERS STOP IN FRONT OF A NEW PARTNER AND THE DANCE BEGINS AGAIN.

Moving to Phrases in American Square Dancing

Before trying the movement, listen for the four phrases

in Section A. Are they all the same length, or different?

same

 Foster: *Camptown Races*

CAMPTOWN RACES

SECTION A

Phrase 1
Ladies to the center and go back home, Doodah, doodah,
(LADIES WALK FOUR STEPS FORWARD, TURN, WALK BACK TO ORIGINAL POSITION.)

Phrase 2
Gents to the center with a right hand star, Oh, doodah day.
(GENTS WALK FORWARD WITH RIGHT HANDS OUTSTRETCHED, TOUCH HANDS IN THE CENTER AND MOVE CLOCKWISE ONCE AROUND THE CIRCLE TO ORIGINAL POSITIONS.)

Phrase 3
Balance in and balance out, Doodah, doodah,
(JOIN LEFT HANDS WITH PARTNER AND RIGHT HANDS WITH CORNER. THE SQUARE BECOMES A CIRCLE WITH LADIES FACING IN AND GENTS FACING OUT. TAKE TWO STEPS FORWARD AND TWO STEPS BACK. DROP RIGHT HANDS. TURN PARTNER AROUND, KEEPING LEFT HANDS JOINED. JOIN RIGHT HANDS WITH NEW PARTNER.)

Phrase 4
Turn with the left hand half about, Oh, doodah day.
(BALANCE IN AND BALANCE OUT. DROP LEFT HANDS WITH ORIGINAL PARTNER AND STAND SIDE BY SIDE WITH NEW PARTNER, READY TO PROMENADE.)

SECTION B 5
Refrain: Promenade
(WALK COUNTERCLOCKWISE AROUND THE CIRCLE AND BACK TO PLACE.)

Early American Dance: Cotton-Eyed Joe

(As taught by Anne Simmons, University of Texas at Arlington)

 Cotton-Eyed Joe

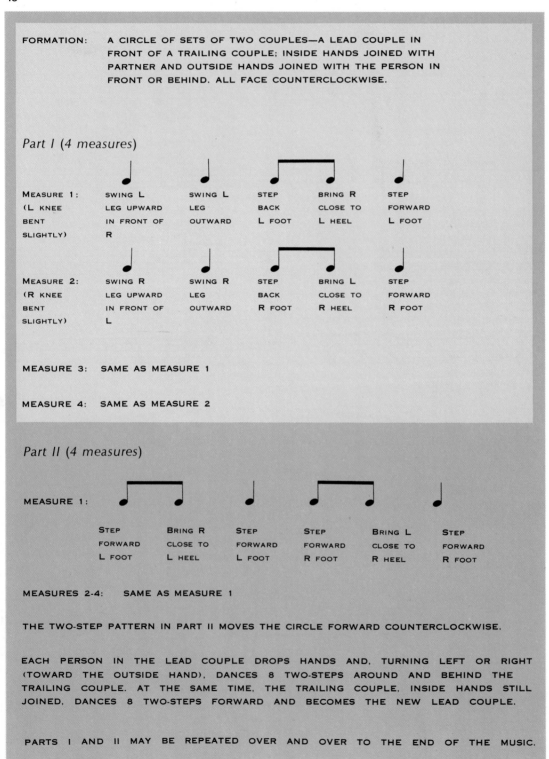

FORMATION: A CIRCLE OF SETS OF TWO COUPLES—A LEAD COUPLE IN FRONT OF A TRAILING COUPLE; INSIDE HANDS JOINED WITH PARTNER AND OUTSIDE HANDS JOINED WITH THE PERSON IN FRONT OR BEHIND. ALL FACE COUNTERCLOCKWISE.

Part I (4 measures)

MEASURE 1: SWING L — SWING L — STEP BACK — BRING R CLOSE TO — STEP FORWARD
(L KNEE BENT SLIGHTLY) — LEG UPWARD IN FRONT OF R — LEG OUTWARD — L FOOT — L HEEL — L FOOT

MEASURE 2: SWING R — SWING R — STEP BACK — BRING L CLOSE TO — STEP FORWARD
(R KNEE BENT SLIGHTLY) — LEG UPWARD IN FRONT OF L — LEG OUTWARD — R FOOT — R HEEL — R FOOT

MEASURE 3: SAME AS MEASURE 1

MEASURE 4: SAME AS MEASURE 2

Part II (4 measures)

MEASURE 1: STEP FORWARD L FOOT — BRING R CLOSE TO L HEEL — STEP FORWARD L FOOT — STEP FORWARD R FOOT — BRING L CLOSE TO R HEEL — STEP FORWARD R FOOT

MEASURES 2-4: SAME AS MEASURE 1

THE TWO-STEP PATTERN IN PART II MOVES THE CIRCLE FORWARD COUNTERCLOCKWISE.

EACH PERSON IN THE LEAD COUPLE DROPS HANDS AND, TURNING LEFT OR RIGHT (TOWARD THE OUTSIDE HAND), DANCES 8 TWO-STEPS AROUND AND BEHIND THE TRAILING COUPLE. AT THE SAME TIME, THE TRAILING COUPLE, INSIDE HANDS STILL JOINED, DANCES 8 TWO-STEPS FORWARD AND BECOMES THE NEW LEAD COUPLE.

PARTS I AND II MAY BE REPEATED OVER AND OVER TO THE END OF THE MUSIC.

The Coal Miner's Song: Miike Tanko

Miike Tanko

Movement patterns

Shoveling Coal (16 beats)

HOLDING AN IMAGINARY SHOVEL WITH BOTH HANDS, MAKE DIGGING MOTIONS. FOOT MOVEMENTS FOLLOW THE STEADY BEAT.

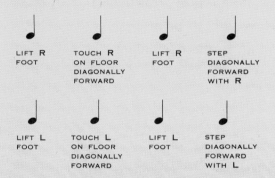

LIFT R FOOT   TOUCH R ON FLOOR DIAGONALLY FORWARD   LIFT R FOOT   STEP DIAGONALLY FORWARD WITH R

LIFT L FOOT   TOUCH L ON FLOOR DIAGONALLY FORWARD   LIFT L FOOT   STEP DIAGONALLY FORWARD WITH L

Carrying coal (12 beats)

HOLD SHOVEL OVER R SHOULDER AND STEP FORWARD WITH R FOOT (2 BEATS). HOLD SHOVEL OVER L SHOULDER AND STEP FORWARD WITH L FOOT (2 BEATS). REPEAT R AND L SHOULDER PATTERNS TWO MORE TIMES.

Looking at the Moon (12 beats)

AS IF LOOKING AT THE MOON, STEP BACKWARD R, RAISING L ARM OVER HEAD AND HOLDING R ARM BEHIND WAIST (2 BEATS).

STEP BACKWARD L, RAISING R ARM AND HOLD L ARM BEHIND WAIST (2 BEATS).

REPEAT R AND L LOOKING-AT-THE-MOON PATTERNS TWO MORE TIMES.

Pushing the Coal Cart (12 beats)

LIFT R KNEE, THEN STEP FORWARD R, MAKING PUSHING MOTION WITH ARMS (2 BEATS).
LIFT L KNEE, THEN STEP FORWARD L, MAKING PUSHING MOTION WITH ARMS (2 BEATS).
REPEAT L AND R PUSHING PATTERN 2 MORE TIMES.

Ending Pattern (8 beats)

BENDING OVER SLIGHTLY FROM THE WAIST, START WITH HANDS CROSSED IN FRONT AND TRACE TWO LARGE CIRCLES BY MOVING EACH ARM OUTWARD TO THE SIDE, UP OVER THE HEAD, AND DOWN TO THE FRONT AGAIN (2 BEATS). CLAP HANDS THREE TIMES (YOI, YOI, YOI) AND GET READY TO BEGIN "SHOVELING COAL" AGAIN.

SAKURA AS DANCED BY SHERRY GEALY

The movements for "Sakura," page 80, help to tell of the beauty of the cherry tree. Each movement is done first to the right and then to the left, filling one phrase of music.

Girls stand in any formation. For the beginning pose, rest right hand on top of left hand at waist level, with both palms up. After each pose in the dance, hands return to the beginning pose. Eyes should follow arm movements in each pose.

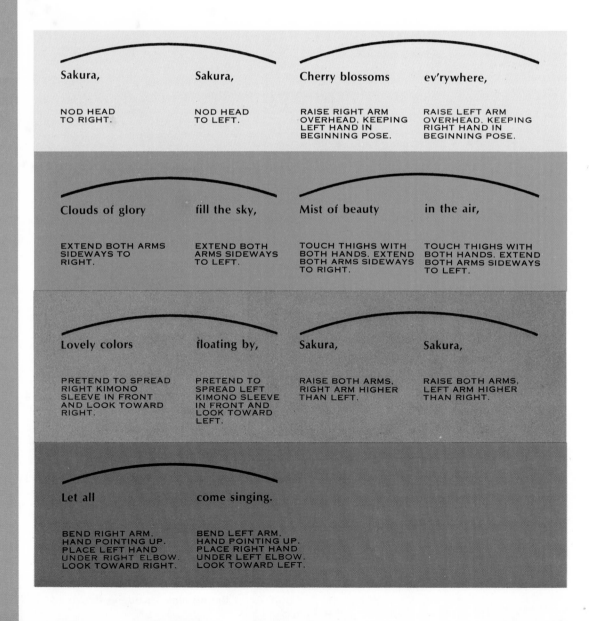

Sakura,

NOD HEAD
TO RIGHT.

Sakura,

NOD HEAD
TO LEFT.

Cherry blossoms

RAISE RIGHT ARM
OVERHEAD, KEEPING
LEFT HAND IN
BEGINNING POSE.

ev'rywhere,

RAISE LEFT ARM
OVERHEAD, KEEPING
RIGHT HAND IN
BEGINNING POSE.

Clouds of glory

EXTEND BOTH ARMS
SIDEWAYS TO
RIGHT.

fill the sky,

EXTEND BOTH
ARMS SIDEWAYS
TO LEFT.

Mist of beauty

TOUCH THIGHS WITH
BOTH HANDS. EXTEND
BOTH ARMS SIDEWAYS
TO RIGHT.

in the air,

TOUCH THIGHS WITH
BOTH HANDS. EXTEND
BOTH ARMS SIDEWAYS
TO LEFT.

Lovely colors

PRETEND TO SPREAD
RIGHT KIMONO
SLEEVE IN FRONT
AND LOOK TOWARD
RIGHT.

floating by,

PRETEND TO
SPREAD LEFT
KIMONO SLEEVE
IN FRONT AND
LOOK TOWARD
LEFT.

Sakura,

RAISE BOTH ARMS,
RIGHT ARM HIGHER
THAN LEFT.

Sakura,

RAISE BOTH ARMS,
LEFT ARM HIGHER
THAN RIGHT.

Let all

BEND RIGHT ARM,
HAND POINTING UP.
PLACE LEFT HAND
UNDER RIGHT ELBOW.
LOOK TOWARD RIGHT.

come singing.

BEND LEFT ARM,
HAND POINTING UP.
PLACE RIGHT HAND
UNDER LEFT ELBOW.
LOOK TOWARD LEFT.

GLOSSARY

absolute music Music that has no suggestion of any nonmusical thing, idea, story, or event (*see* program music).

accent A single tone or chord louder than those around it.

accompaniment Music that supports the sound of a solo performer.

atonal Music in which no single tone is a "home base" or "resting place."

ballad In music, a song that tells a story.

beat A repeating pulse that can be felt in some music.

cadence A group of chords or notes at the end of a phrase or piece that gives a feeling of pausing or finishing.

call and response A musical device with a portion of a melody (call) followed by an answering portion (response). The response may imitate the call or it may be a separate melody that repeats each time.

canon A device in which a melody begins in one part, and then is imitated by other parts in an overlapping fashion (*see* round).

chant To sing in a manner approximating speech.

chord Three or more different tones played or sung together.

chord pattern An arrangement of chords into a small grouping, usually occurring often in a piece.

chorus (*See* refrain.)

clef A sign that tells where pitches are located on the staff. The sign 𝄞 (G clef, or treble clef) shows that G above middle C is on the second line. This clef is used for music in higher registers. The sign 𝄢 (F clef, or bass clef) shows the tone F below middle C on the fourth line. It is used for music in lower registers.

cluster A group of tones very close together performed at the same time; used mostly in modern music.

composer A person who makes up pieces of music by putting sounds together in his or her own way.

contour The "shape" of a melody, made by the way it moves upward and downward in steps and leaps, and by repeated tones.

contrast Two or more things that are different. In music, slow is a *contrast* to fast; section A is a *contrast* to section B.

countermelody A melody that is played or sung at the same time as the main melody.

density The thickness or thinness of sound.

duration The length of sounds, from very short to very long.

dynamics The loudness and softness of sounds.

elements The parts out of which whole works of art are made: for example, music uses the *elements* melody, rhythm, texture, tone color, form; painting uses line, color, space, shape, etc.

ensemble A group of players or singers.

fermata A sign (⌢) indicating that a note is held longer than its written note value, stopping or "holding" the beat.

frets Strips of metal across the fingerboard of guitars and similar instruments. The player raises the pitch of a string by pressing it into contact with a fret.

form The overall plan of a piece of music.

fugue A musical procedure based on imitation, in which the main melody (subject) and related melodies are repeated in higher and lower registers and in different keys. The texture is polyphonic.

ground A melody pattern repeated over and over in the bass (lowest part) of a piece, while other things happen above it.

harmony Two or more tones sounding at the same time.

improvisation Making up music as it is being performed; often used in jazz.

interval The distance between tones. The smallest interval in traditional Western music is the half-step (f–f$^\sharp$, f$^\sharp$–g, etc.), but contemporary music and music of other cultures often use smaller intervals.

jazz A style that grew out of the music of black Americans, then took many different substyles—ragtime, blues, cool jazz, swing, bebop, rock, etc.

key The particular scale on which a piece of music or section is based, named for its tonic, or key-tone, or "home-base" tone. (The key of D major indicates that the major scale starting and ending on the tone D is being used. *See* tonality.)

major scale An arrangement of eight tones in a scale according to the following intervals, or steps: whole, whole, half, whole, whole, whole, half.

251

measure A grouping of beats set off by bar lines.

melody A line of single tones that move upward, downward, or repeat.

melody pattern An arrangement of pitches into a small grouping, usually occurring often in a piece.

meter The way the beats of music are grouped, often in sets of two or in sets of three. The meter signature, or time signature, such as $\frac{3}{4}$ or $\frac{4}{4}$, tells how many beats are in the group, or measure (top number), and the kind of note that gets one beat (bottom number).

minor scale Several arrangements of eight tones in a scale, such as *natural minor* (whole, half, whole, whole, half, whole, whole) and *melodic minor* (upward: whole, half, whole, whole, whole, whole, half; downward: whole, whole, half, whole, whole, half, whole).

notes Symbols for sound in music.

octave The distance of eight steps from one tone to another that has the same letter name. On the staff these steps are shown by the lines and spaces. When notes are an *octave* apart, there are eight lines and spaces from one note to the other.

ornamentation In the arts, the addition of decorations, or embellishments, to the basic structure of the work.

ostinato A rhythmic or melodic phrase that keeps repeating throughout a piece or a section of a piece.

pattern In the arts, an arrangement of an element or elements into a grouping, usually occurring often in the work (see elements).

phrase A musical sentence. Each *phrase* expresses one thought. Music is made up of *phrases* that follow one another in a way that sounds right.

pitch The highness or lowness of a tone.

polyrhythm Several different rhythm patterns going on at the same time, often causing conflicts of meter among them.

program music Music that suggests or describes some nonmusical idea, story, or event (see absolute music).

range In a melody, the span from the lowest tone to the highest tone.

refrain A part of a song that repeats, with the same music and words. It is often called the "chorus," since it is usually sung by all the singers, while the verses in between are often sung by one voice.

register The pitch location of a group of tones (see pitch). If the group of tones are all high sounds, they are in a high *register*. If the group of tones are all low sounds, they are in a low *register*.

repetition Music that is the same, or almost the same, as music that was heard earlier.

rests Symbols for silences in music.

rhythm The way movement is organized in a piece of music, using beat, no beat, long and short sounds, meter, accents, no accents, tempo, syncopation, etc.

rhythm pattern A pattern of long and short sounds.

rondo A musical form in which a section is repeated, with contrasting sections in between (such as A B A C A).

round A kind of canon that leads back to the beginning of the melody and starts all over again (circle canon).

scale An arrangement of pitches from lower to higher according to a specific pattern of intervals. Major, minor, pentatonic, whole-tone, and chromatic are five kinds of scales. Each one has its own arrangement of pitches.

sequence The repetition of a melody pattern at a higher or lower pitch level.

solo Music for a single player or singer, often with an accompaniment.

staff A set of five horizontal lines on which music notes are written.

style The overall effect a work of art makes by the way its elements are used (see elements). When works of art use elements similarly, they are said to be "in the same style."

subject See fugue.

syncopation An arrangement of rhythm in which prominent or important tones begin on weak beats or weak parts of beats, giving a catchy, off-balance movement to the music.

tempo The speed of the beat in a piece of music (see beat).

texture The way melody and harmony go together: a melody alone, two or more melodies together, or a melody with chords.

theme An important melody that occurs several times in a piece of music.

tonal Music that focuses on one tone that is more important than the others—a "home base"—or resting tone.

tonality The kind of scale, major or minor, on which a piece of music or section is based (see key).

tone color The special sound that makes one instrument or voice sound different from another.

tone row An arrangement of the twelve tones of the chromatic scale into a series in which there is no focus on any one of them as the home tone. When the series is played backward, it is called the "retrograde."

triplet A rhythm pattern made by dividing a beat into three equal sounds.

variation Music that is repeated but changed in some important way.

INDEX

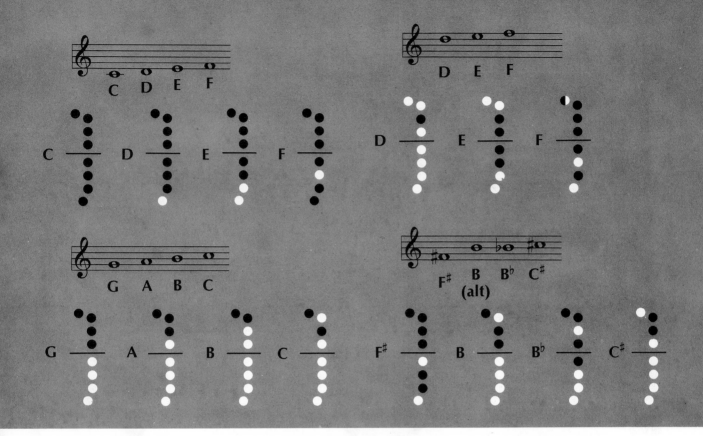

PICTURE CREDITS

3 4 5 6 7 8 9 10—RRD—88 87 86 85 84 83 82